ISAIAH AND THE ASSYRIAN CRISIS

STUDIES IN BIBLICAL THEOLOGY

A series of monographs designed to provide clergy and laymen with the best work in biblical scholarship both in this country and abroad

STUDIES IN BIBLICAL THEOLOGY

Second Series · 3

ISAIAH AND
THE ASSYRIAN CRISIS

BREVARD S. CHILDS

SCM PRESS LTD

BLOOMSBURY STREET LONDON

FIRST PUBLISHED 1967
© SCM PRESS LTD 1967
PRINTED IN GREAT BRITAIN BY
ROBERT CUNNINGHAM AND SONS LTD
ALVA

CONTENTS

PREFACE

THIS monograph grew out of a seminar on the message of Isaiah. It soon became evident to me that the events which climaxed in the Assyrian invasion of 701 were of decisive importance, and that one's whole image of the prophet depended on how one judged his relation to this crisis. Yet the historical problems connected with Sennacherib's attack seemed hopelessly locked in a scholarly impasse. As a result, various sets of categories have been employed—historical, literary, theological, and psychological—by which to organize the material and explain the prophet's message. Often these lacked exegetical control and were rooted more in the interpreter than in the texts being interpreted.

This study approaches the problem from a different vantage point. An attempt is made, first of all, to trace the various levels within the history of the Isaianic tradition before attacking the historical problems as such. By analysing the various ways in which Israel reacted to her traditions a new perspective is opened into the historical and theological message of the prophet which is sensitive to the tension, interaction, and resolution of elements which together constitute the full biblical witness.

I wish to express my appreciation to several friends for valuable assistance. J. Donald Shenkel of Woodstock College offered aid on several text critical problems. J. William Whedbee of Pomona College read the entire manuscript and contributed many valuable insights. Finally, I am indebted to my wife, Ann, for encouragement, good humour, and wisdom.

B. S. C.

New Haven, Conn.
February 24, 1967

ABBREVIATIONS

AJSL	*American Journal of Semitic Languages and Literatures*
*ANET*²	J. B. Pritchard, *Ancient Near Eastern Texts relating to the Old Testament*², 1955
BA	*The Biblical Archaeologist*
BASOR	*Bulletin of the American Schools of Oriental Research*
BH	*Biblia Hebraica*, ed. Rudolf Kittel, 3rd ed., A. Alt and O. Eissfeldt, 1952
BJRL	*Bulletin of the John Rylands Library*
CBQ	*Catholic Biblical Quarterly*
GSAT	*Gesammelte Studien zum Alten Testament*
HTR	*Harvard Theological Review*
ICC	International Critical Commentary
IDB	*Interpreter's Dictionary of the Bible*
JBL	*Journal of Biblical Literature*
JE	*Jewish Encyclopaedia*
JQR	*Jewish Quarterly Review*
JSS	*Journal of Semitic Studies*
JTS	*Journal of Theological Studies*
*KS*²	A. Alt, *Kleine Schriften zur Geschichte des Volkes Israel*, 1953
LXX	Greek Translation of the Old Testament (Septuagint)
MT	Masoretic text
OIP	Oriental Institute Publications
PJ	*Palästinajahrbuch*
RB	*Revue Biblique*
RGG	*Die Religion in Geschichte und Gegenwart*
SAT	*Die Schriften des Alten Testaments in Auswahl*
SJT	*Scottish Journal of Theology*
ThZ	*Theologische Zeitschrift*
TLZ	*Theologische Literaturzeitung*
VT	*Vetus Testamentum*
ZAW	*Zeitschrift für die alttestamentliche Wissenschaft*

I

THE NATURE OF THE PROBLEM

FEW problems within the Old Testament have evoked such a steady stream of monographs and articles as has the account of the Assyrian invasion of Palestine in 701 BC.[1] It has become a classic issue on which each new generation of biblical scholars seems constrained to test its mettle. The reasons why this problem has not been allowed to rest, but continues to offer its challenge are not difficult to discover. In the first place, there are so many accounts of Sennacherib's invasion and they are given in such detail within the Bible that the event has assumed an importance by its very frequency. The incident is first recounted in II Kings 18.13-16. It appears again in II Kings 18.17-19.37 in a passage which appears to contain two parallel sources of the one incident.[2] This latter account is duplicated with minor variations in Isa. 36.1-37.38. Then again, II Chron. 32.1-23 deals with the same subject. Finally, there are numerous allusions to the incident in the book of Isaiah and elsewhere.[3] Naturally the problem of understanding the relationship of these various accounts becomes immediately acute.

Secondly, the history of the Assyrian invasion is recorded also in the annals of Sennacherib which have been preserved in various editions and copies.[4] The expedition of 701 into Palestine belongs

[1] The literature on the subject is too vast to list. Most of the important books and articles will be mentioned in the ensuing discussion. The following provide the best bibliographical survey: Leo L. Honor, *Sennacherib's Invasion of Palestine* (New York, 1926); J. A. Montgomery, *The Books of Kings* (ICC, Edinburgh, 1951), pp. 513f.; H. Tadmor, 'Hezekiah', *Encyclopaedia Biblica* (Hebrew), III (Jerusalem, 1958), p. 99; H. H. Rowley, 'Hezekiah's Reform and Rebellion', *BJRL* 44 (1962), pp. 395ff.

[2] The problem of sources will be treated in ch. III.

[3] Cf. O. Eissfeldt, 'Ezechiel als Zeuge für Sanheribs Eingriff in Palästina', *Kleine Schriften*, I (Tübingen, 1962), pp. 239ff.

[4] A thorough discussion of the Assyrian sources is given by Honor, *op. cit.*, pp. 1ff. Cf. also the analysis of C. van Leeuwen, 'Sennachérib devant Jérusalem', *Oudtest. Studiën* XIV, pp. 245ff. The most convenient collection of texts is given by D. D. Luckenbill, *The Annals of Sennacherib* (OIP II, Chicago,

to his third campaign. The Assyrian account not only mentions the attack on the coastal cities, but also makes an explicit reference to Hezekiah, the siege of Jerusalem, and the tribute exacted from him at his submission. The perennial problem lies in establishing the relation between the Assyrian sources and the various biblical accounts. The question is particularly intriguing to the historian because seldom is a biblical story augmented by such a detailed source which is not only contemporary to the event, but which also reflects a point of view outside of the Hebrew community.

Thirdly, the solution of this problem has profound implications for the interpretation of the book of Isaiah, and even for one's understanding of the role of prophet in general. What is the relation between the oracles of Isaiah and the stories about the prophet? How was Isaiah's message understood by later generations? For these reasons, every generation of Bible commentators has focused attention on the problem.

In spite of this concentrated scholarly activity, a definite impasse appears to have been reached. No consensus has developed regarding the historical problems of the invasion; in fact, opinion continues to diverge as much as ever. The historical evidence which is needed to understand the actual historical sequence of events appears to be unavailable. As a result, every hypothetical reconstruction rests upon enough unproven assumptions to prevent the degree of historical probability needed to form a consensus. This point can be made clearer by reviewing the major solutions which have been offered.

The first theory attempts to reconstruct the events according to the order of the biblical narratives. That is to say, the submission of Hezekiah to Sennacherib, as recorded in II Kings 18.14-16 with its close parallel in the Assyrian annals, is followed by a subsequent encounter in which Sennacherib's attempt to conquer Jerusalem is repulsed (II Kings 18.17ff.). According to this theory, the Assyrian victories over the coastal cities convinced Hezekiah that resistance was hopeless and he sued for peace. Sennacherib placed upon him a heavy tribute, but left the city intact. Then later—and various reasons are offered as explanations

---

1924). The most recent translation of the Oriental Institute prism is by A. Leo Oppenheim, *ANET*[2], pp. 287f. A selection from the well-known Taylor prism is found in D. Winton Thomas, ed., *Documents from Old Testament Times* (London, 1958), pp. 66f.

—the Assyrian king changed his mind and demanded complete capitulation and surrender of the city. Hezekiah, encouraged by Isaiah, refused to comply in the face of the threats. Then quite suddenly Sennacherib was forced to withdraw leaving the city untouched.

This reconstruction has much in its favour, and it continues to be defended by a large number of scholars with new variations.[5] The theory can claim *prima facie* support from the text in II Kings 18-19, or more exactly from the redactor of these chapters, who suggests by his juxtaposition of 18.14-16 to vv. 17ff. a sequence of events. Again, this interpretation allows for the possibility of combining the testimony of Hezekiah's surrender, which has the clearest confirmation in II Kings 18.13-16 and in the Assyrian annals, with the latter account in Kings and elsewhere of the Assyrian's defeat and of Jerusalem's deliverance. Moreover, it offers a plausible explanation for the growth of the tradition of Zion's inviolability in terms of the escape in 701. Finally, it can fit many elements of the story in 18.17ff. which would appear to reflect genuine historical tradition into a reasonable pattern such as the Assyrian emissary from Lachish (v. 17), the insolent refusal to speak Aramaic (vv. 26f.), the rumour of an Egyptian force (19.9), etc.

However, this reconstruction suffers from several obvious weaknesses which critics have frequently pointed out.[6] First of all, the value of the alleged testimony in II Kings 18f. to a sequence of events is called into question by the presence of two sources in vv. 18ff. which are, by and large, parallel, and which have been secondarily linked together by a redactor in 19.9. Similarly, the twenty year interval between the return of Sennacherib from Jerusalem and his death in 681 is not reflected in 19.36f. Again, a serious objection to the above theory is that there is no connection made in the text between the account in 18.14-16 and the account in 17ff. when, in fact, a reference to the earlier surrender would

---

[5] J. Meinhold, *Die Jesajaerzählungen* (Göttingen, 1898), pp. 99ff.; R. Kittel, *Geschichte des Volkes Israel*[7], II (Stuttgart, 1925), pp. 430ff.; R. de Vaux, *Supplément au Dictionnaire de la Bible*, IV (1949), pp. 755f.; J. Scharbert, *Die Propheten Israels bis 700 v. Chr.* (Köln, 1965), pp. 288ff.; B. Mazar, 'Sennacherib's Judaean Campaign', *The Military History of the Land of Israel in Biblical Times* (Hebrew), ed. J. Liver (Tel Aviv, 1965), pp. 291ff.

[6] Cf. the criticism of J. Bright, *A History of Israel* (Philadelphia, 1959 and London, 1960), pp. 284f.

have been expected. This theory rests, therefore, in large measure
upon providing a motivation for Sennacherib's subsequent
attitude which has no support in the text itself.[7] Moreover, the
theory encounters difficulty in interpreting certain of Isaiah's
oracles which imply defeat and dishonour (1.5ff.; 22.1ff.). Finally,
there are details within the Assyrian annals and the biblical
accounts which do not fit easily into the reconstruction, such as
the anachronism of the name Tirhakah,[8] and the need for 'another'
Egyptian army to cause the final Assyrian withdrawal.

The second major theory of reconstruction tries to fit the
sequence of events within the framework of the account in
18.14-16 with its close Assyrian parallel. There is a good bit of
variation within the theory on how to interpret 18.17ff. This
depends on the amount of historical validity which the individual
commentator attributes to the second source. Some commentators
tend to dismiss the account in 18.17ff. as having little historical
value,[9] while others regard it as reflecting much that is historical.[10]
However, the feature common to all within this group is the
conviction that the final action of the campaign was the capitulation of Hezekiah with the subsequent payment of the tribute
demanded in 18.14-16.

This second reconstruction also has some very strong points
to commend it. First of all, it has tried to take seriously the
different qualities exhibited within the various source materials,
and right from the start to exercise a critical judgment in making
use of these sources.[11] The reconstruction is based on a sound
historical principle: one begins with the most reliable evidence in
forming a judgment and then moves into areas in which the
degree of historical probability is much smaller. Again, this

[7] A frequent device is to speak of 'Sennacherib's treachery', and use
Isa. 33.1, 8 for support, e.g. W. Robertson Smith, *The Prophets of Israel*[2]
(London, 1895), pp. 350ff.; Kittel, *op. cit.*, p. 435; Scharbert, *op. cit.*, p. 288.

[8] For the problem of Tirhakah, cf. W. F. Albright, *BASOR* 130 (1953),
pp. 8ff.; J. M. A. Janssen, 'Que sait-on actuellement du Pharaon Taharqa?',
Biblica 34 (1953), pp. 23ff.; S. H. Horn, 'Did Sennacherib campaign once or
twice against Hezekiah?', *Andrews Univ. Seminary Studies*, IV (1966), pp. 3ff.

[9] A. Alt, *Israel und Aegypten* (Leipzig, 1909), pp. 79f.; W. Rudolph, 'San-
herib in Palästina', *PJ* 25 (1929), pp. 74f.; M. Noth, *The History of Israel*[2]
(London, 1960), p. 268; S. H. Blank, *Prophetic Faith in Isaiah* (New York and
London, 1958), pp. 12ff.

[10] A. Parrot, *Nineveh and the Old Testament* (New York and London, 1955),
pp. 56ff.

[11] Rudolph, *op. cit.*, p. 74.

hypothesis accords well with the historical situation of Judah and Palestine in general, subsequent to the invasion of 701. It offers a plausible basis for understanding Isaiah's oracles of judgment in chapters 1, 22, 30 etc. Finally, this interpretation of the sources explains adequately many of the details contained in the sources, such as why Hezekiah was allowed to continue as king with only the loss of his territory,[12] or why the Assyrians could confidently expect the tribute to be sent to Nineveh after the capitulation.

Again there are difficulties and weak points which cause the theory to appear to many as far from convincing. The most frequently argued point of dissention lies in explaining how the tradition of Jerusalem's deliverance (18.17ff), could have been sustained in the face of an abject defeat. How was it possible for the tradition of Zion's inviolability to have been cherished and even to have grown in the light of this interpretation of the events? Once again, if the accounts in 18.17ff. are discounted as legendary, then one is faced with the problem of accounting for the elements which do seem to be genuinely historical. If one attempts to evaluate these elements in a positive way and to fit them within the framework of 18.14-16, then unexpressed motivations must be supplied to link the stories together. Then the same methodological difficulty which was raised against the first theory of reconstruction recurs. Finally, there are numerous questions which remain. Is it likely that the Assyrian annals would have recorded a defeat if one had occurred? If Sennacherib had been as successful as the annals suggest against Hezekiah and the Egyptians at Eltekeh, why did he not press his victory into Egypt? Why was Hezekiah treated with a leniency which was in striking contrast to the other less important rebels? Or were there reasons which forced the Assyrians to withdraw suddenly as suggested in 19.9, 35ff.?

The third reconstruction attempts to avoid the problems inherent in the former by positing two separate invasions by Sennacherib which have not been clearly distinguished in the biblical accounts. Accordingly, the first occurred in 701 and is listed in the Assyrian annals as Sennacherib's third campaign. The second occurred sometime after 690. The first attack resulted in the victory of the Assyrians and the abject submission of Hezekiah,

---

[12] A. Alt, 'Nachwort über die territorialgeschichtliche Bedeutung von Sanheribs Eingriff in Palästina', *PJ* 25 (1929), pp. 8off. = *KS²*, 242ff.

whereas in the second invasion the Assyrians suffered an unexpected setback and Jerusalem was spared. The account in
18.14-16 is assigned to the invasion of 701. There is some disagreement over whether both of the parallel accounts in 18.17ff.
belong to the second invasion or whether only one of the emissary
stories does, but at least one of the latter sources is always assigned
to the later event.

There are some obvious strengths to this interpretation which
continues to gain support in growing numbers in the English
speaking world.[13] First of all, the theory of two historically
separated invasions provides a clear explanation as to why there
is a tradition of defeat and also a tradition of deliverance. The
need to supply a psychological link between these two events has
been eliminated. Again, the theory makes plausible the apparent
tension within Isaiah's oracles which fluctuate between words of
immanent disaster for Israel and assured promises of rescue from
Assyria's threats. Moreover, the causes of the subsequent growth
of the Zion tradition become clear on the ground of the remarkable deliverance to which is attributed a similar historical veracity
as that afforded the earlier defeat. Finally, within the theory is
offered an explanation of several details which were especially
bothersome in the other reconstructions. For example, the
reference to Tirhakah is no longer an embarrassing anachronism,
but is assigned to the second campaign of c.689, at which time
Tirhakah had assumed rule in Egypt. Similarly, the assassination
of Sennacherib in 681 is brought into closer proximity with the
second departure from Palestine.

However, there are several major problems which have not
been met with full satisfaction.[14] The first objection raised against
the two invasion theory is the difficulty of establishing the fact of a
second Assyrian campaign into Palestine. Since there is no evidence for this enterprise in the years covered by the annals of
Sennacherib, the usual attempt has been to assign it to the period

---

[13] H. Winckler, *Alttestamentliche Untersuchungen* (Leipzig, 1892), pp. 28ff.;
K. Fullerton, 'The Invasion of Sennacherib', *Bibliotheca Sacra* 63 (1906),
pp. 577ff.; W. Staerk, *Das assyrische Weltreich im Urteil der Propheten* (Göttingen,
1908), pp. 81ff.; R. W. Rogers, 'Sennacherib and Judah', *Wellhausen Festschrift*
(Giessen, 1914), pp. 319ff.; W. F. Albright, *BASOR*, 130 (1953), pp. 8ff., and
140 (1956), pp. 25f.; J. Bright, *A History of Israel*, pp. 282ff., and in the
Vischer Festschrift; S. H. Horn, *op. cit.*, pp. 1ff.

[14] Cf. the criticism of H. H. Rowley, *op. cit.*, pp. 407ff.

following the last campaign of the annals, which is sometime after 690. Two arguments have been adduced to support this dating: (*a*) the reference to a subsequent Arabic campaign on a broken alabaster slab,[15] and (*b*) the story in Herodotus (II, 141) concerning the field mice who crippled the Assyrian army at the border of Egypt. Both of these arguments are at best tenuous,[16] and raise as many problems as they resolve. Moreover, the attempt to set Hezekiah's death as late as 686 is also faced with real problems.[17]

Again, the theory of two separate invasions finds little support from the text itself. There is no internal evidence which would point to an alleged telescoping. The theory seems to reflect the same harmonistic method employed in explaining the repetition in the Synoptic Gospels by positing different events to which the parallels are referred. Moreover, the fact that there is rather strong disagreement among the defenders of the theory as to which biblical accounts constitute the first invasion and which the second would emphasize the artificial nature of the separation. Then again, many question whether this historical reconstruction does in fact provide the key for interpreting the tension within the oracles of Isaiah. The attempt to assign his prophecies of judgment and those of salvation to separate periods cannot be carried through convincingly.[18] Rather, the polarity of the prophet's thought seems to be of a different kind than that envisioned by those employing this historical theory as a key. Finally, there are numerous points in the accounts which are not convincingly answered by the theory. For example, is it likely that Sennacherib would have established his base twice at Lachish, and why is there no reference to the earlier defeat in the threat of the Rabshakeh (18.19ff.; 19.1off.)?

While any number of combinations[19] of the above reconstruc-

---

[15] Berlin Museum, V.A. 3310 published in *Vorderasiatische Schriftdenkmäler* I, No. 77, and by Luckenbill, *op. cit.*, pp. 89ff. Cf. the additional notes by Rogers, *op. cit.*, p. 327 and Honor, *op. cit.*, pp. 11, 30.

[16] On the question of the Berlin fragment, cf. A. Alt, *Assyrer und Aethiopen*, (Leipzig, 1909), pp. 81f.; and A. L. Oppenheim, 'Sennacherib', *IDB*, IV, p. 272. On the question of the Herodotus legend, cf. the bibliography in ch. III, p. 101.

[17] Cf. the summary of the problem in Rowley, *op. cit.*, pp. 409ff., and the discussion by Tadmor, *op. cit.*, pp. 97ff.

[18] Cf. the discussion of Isaiah's oracles in ch. II.

[19] For example, H. Haag, 'La Campagne de Sennachérib contre Jérusalem en 701', *RB* 58 (1958), pp. 348ff., who attempts to combine the reference to the retreat of Sennacherib before the rumour of the Egyptian army (II Kings

tions have been attempted, these have not succeeded principally in presenting another fresh alternative. Therefore, there seems to be no need to discuss other variations in detail.

To summarize: a survey of the major theories by which the events have been reconstructed illustrates the impasse which has been reached regarding the problem. It would seem that no one theory has been able to marshal a consensus, which, of course, was the thesis propounded forty years ago by Honor.[20]

The purpose of this monograph is to suggest that, in spite of the present impasse, an important dimension of the problem has never been adequately investigated. No thorough form critical study of the biblical accounts has been attempted. Occasional statements of a form critical nature have often been made, but without a concentrated endeavour to pursue the issue consistently from this perspective. Whether this method can succeed in breaking the impasse outlined above remains to be seen. Perhaps such a study will only succeed in making more precise why the impasse cannot be broken on the basis of the present sources. Nevertheless, a form critical study should have important implications for several aspects of the problem.

First of all, in respect to the *historical* problem, a form critical study should clarify the exact nature of the sources which have been used for a historical reconstruction. While an examination of one's sources seems an obvious imperative for critical historiography, this task has not been carried through in point of fact. The tendency has been either to treat all the biblical passages on a similar plane of historical verisimilitude,[21] or to subject them to broad categories such as 'legend', with an implied value judgment regarding historicity.[22] When, on occasion, precise distinctions

---

19.7-9) with the massacre of his troops 'by the angel of Yahweh' (19.35). Both from a literary and historical point of view this reconstruction is not convincing.

[20] L. Honor, *op. cit.*, p. xiv.

[21] John Bright's method appears extremely vulnerable at this point. He writes concerning II Kings 18.17-19.37: 'The account not only contains various allusions to the events of the ninth and eighth centuries that can be checked from Assyrian records, it also exhibits no really legendary features at all. . . .' (*History* . . ., p. 283). To assume with Albright that the reference to the destruction of famous cities during the preceding centuries demonstrates the historical nature of the whole account is a startling *non sequitur*. In his debate with his opponents Bright deals with the biblical text very much as he would a modern newspaper account (pp. 284ff.).

[22] Blank, *op. cit.*, pp. 9ff.

between the accounts have been attempted, only the restricted methods of earlier literary criticism have been operative.[23]

Secondly, in respect to the *literary* problem, a form critical study should provide a basis for understanding the development of Israel's traditions from the early oral stages, through written formulation, to its final incorporation into larger historical works. Even if the historical problem proves in the end again to be insoluble in the light of the evidence, this does not preclude an understanding of how Israel's traditions regarding the events developed. It cannot be emphasized strongly enough that the problem in the history of tradition is distinct from the problem of determining historicity. The failure to recognize the distinction between history and tradition has led to all kinds of dubious psychological and historical conjectures when it comes to the problem of *Traditionsgeschichte*.

Finally, in respect to the *theological* problem, a form critical study should be especially important in clarifying the different expressions of Israel's faith toward the Assyrian threat. It may be possible to trace the growth and reformulation of the tradition in the light of a later perspective. But the theological task cannot be carried through with precision until the texts are freed from methods of apologetic harmonization, sterile rationalism, or historical reductionism.[24] A serious wrestling with the problem of how to deal with such a variety of different responses within one historic community is needed. We must resist the easy categories of religious development or *heilsgeschichtliche* schematization. It remains to be seen whether one can attain a full control of the complex minutiae of the problem and at the same time offer a satisfactory synthesis of the theological issues. The disadvantages of attempting a monograph on such a restricted subject can be justified if the results of the study succeed in illuminating a number of similar problems at the same time.

[23] J. Meinhold, *op. cit.*, pp. 27ff., 74ff.
[24] To assume with many that the reference in 19.35 to the 'angel of Yahweh who slew 185,000' is a reference to the bubonic plague carried by mice prevents any serious theological reflection on the tradition at the outset.

II

THE ORACLES OF ISAIAH

An examination of the eighth century prophet constitutes the logical place to begin a study of the tradition of Isaiah and the Assyrians. Because the words of Isaiah as they now appear in the Hebrew Bible have passed through a long and complicated history of transmission with much editing and reworking, one of the essential tasks of the form critical analyst will be to determine, as closely as possible, the primary level of Isaianic tradition in respect to the Assyrian crisis of 701. The intention to focus the study on this one subject during the later ministry of Isaiah is not always easy to realize. The effort to date a passage in Isaiah precisely is often impossible. Often one must be satisfied with an approximation. It seems also necessary to treat several passages which precede the actual crisis because of their significance in providing the historical background. Any such attempt to limit the scope of the study to one period must be somewhat arbitrary, but it is to be hoped that the distortion will not be a fundamental one.

A. THE INVECTIVE-THREAT

1. Isaiah 1.4-9[1]

4. Woe, sinful nation, people heavy with guilt,
   Seed of evil-doers, children who deal corruptly!
   They have forsaken Yahweh, they have spurned the Holy One
   of Israel,
   They are completely estranged.

5. Why will you still be smitten in continuing to revolt?
   The whole head is sick, and the whole heart ill.

---

[1] Text criticism of 1.4-9: V.4, the final two words may be a gloss. V.7, emend the second *zārîm* with *BH*. Cf. the recent suggestion by S. Speier, *ThZ* 21 (1965), p. 310.

6. From the sole of the foot to the crown there is no sound spot
   in it,
   Only bruises and welts and fresh wounds;
   They have not been closed, nor bandaged,
   Nor softened with oil.

7. Your land is a desolation, your cities are gutted with fire;
   Aliens devour your land in your very presence,
   It is desolate like the overthrow of (Sodom).

8. And the daughter of Zion is left like a booth in a vineyard,
   Like a hut in a cucumber field, like a besieged city.

9. If Yahweh of Hosts had not left us a few survivors,
   We would have become like Sodom and resembled Gomorrah.

At first sight this passage seems to fit into the classical pattern of the invective-threat.[2] The oracle is spoken by the prophet which sets it off from the Yahweh speech of vv. 2-3. The invective begins with the typical woe (*hôy*)[3] exclamation and is closely attached to the addressee of the reproach who is first described in a series of nominal clauses. These clauses serve to establish the cause for the rebuke and issue in the threat which follows. Wolff[4] has convincingly made the point that these two aspects of the oracle are not separate forms, but belong integrally together. The rhetorical questions are typical for the reproach, but assume an even greater magnitude in Isaiah.

Nevertheless, it is somewhat surprising to find that the usual threat pattern diverges from the expected. The reproach does not

---

[2] The terminology of *Scheltrede-Drohwort* was introduced into O.T. studies by H. Gunkel. Cf. his articles in *RGG*¹ IV, pp. 1875ff., and in *Die Grossen Propheten*², *SAT* II, 2, pp. xxxivff. The distinction was further refined by E. Balla, *Die Droh- und Scheltworte des Amos* (Leipzig, 1926). H. W. Wolff offered several important modifications in his important article, 'Die Begründungen der prophetischen Heils- und Unheilssprüche', *ZAW* 52 (1934), pp. 1ff. = *GSAT*, pp. 9ff. More recent discussions are by R. B. Y. Scott, 'The Literary Structure of Isaiah's Oracles', *Studies in Old Testament Prophecy* (Edinburgh, 1950), pp. 179ff.; C. Westermann, *Grundformen prophetischer Rede* (München, 1960); R. Rendtorff, *RGG*³ V, pp. 635ff.

[3] E. Gerstenberger, 'The Woe-Oracles of the Prophets', *JBL* 81 (1962), pp. 249ff. has offered a major new insight which is a convincing reply to Westermann, *op. cit.*, pp. 137ff. Cf. Wolff's acceptance, *Amos' Geistige Heimat* (Neukirchen, 1964), pp. 12ff. The antipodal relationship between *'ašrê* and *hôy* has been recently contested by W. Janzen, *HTR* 58 (1965), pp. 215ff., but see G. Wanke, *ZAW* 78 (1966), pp. 215ff.

[4] Wolff, 'Die Begründungen', *op. cit.*, pp. 1ff.

issue into a message of impending judgment[5] which is delivered in a Yahweh speech. Rather, the judgment has already fallen and Israel still partakes of it. The prophet continues to vary his illustration to emphasize the extent and seriousness of the present condition. The sickness is total; the shame is absolute; the condition is desperate! The concluding lament[6] makes it clear that the expected threat has not developed. Instead, the tone of the passage rings with the notes of a lament. The complaint of rejection, defeat, and shame are all familiar from the Psalter. However, these are now directed, not to God, but to Israel with whom the prophet identifies (v. 9).

Most commentators are agreed regarding the background of this oracle. It reflects a period closely following the assault of the Assyrians in 701. The country has been overrun by the enemy and desolated. Only Jerusalem, the daughter of Zion, is left isolated and exposed in the midst of disaster.[7] The people who have been spared are not 'a holy remnant', but very much the sinful nation whom the prophet admonishes in terms of lament and urges to cease from their insane folly of self destruction. The impact of the concrete historical predicament bears the main responsibility for having fractured the traditional prophetic form.[8]

2. Isaiah 22.1-14[9]

1. What is the matter with you that all of you have gone up on the rooftops?

[5] Gerstenberger's characterization of the introductory woe is certainly correct (*op. cit.*, p. 251): 'They seek to describe a person or group of persons in regard to what they are doing.'

[6] It is necessary to distinguish between 'woe oracles' and laments (*contra* G. E. Wright, 'The Nations in Hebrew Prophecy', *Encounter* 26 (1965), pp. 233f.). The lament as *Klage* has been described by Gunkel-Begrich, *Einleitung in die Psalmen* (Göttingen, 1933), pp. 117ff. The lament as *Leichenlied* (dirge) has been given a classical treatment by H. Jahnow, *Das Hebräische Leichenlied* (Giessen, 1923). The sharp form critical lines should not be blurred unnecessarily.

[7] The striking parallel to the Assyrian annal has often been cited in this connection. 'As for Hezekiah, the Jew ... forty-six of his strong walled towers and innumerable smaller villages ... I besieged and conquered ... I made to come out from them 200, 150 people, young and old ... innumerable horses, mules etc. . . . He himself I shut up like a caged bird within Jerusalem. . . .' *ANET*[2], p. 288, or Thomas, *op. cit.*, p. 67.

[8] The question to what extent other factors may well have been involved must be left open. The Near Eastern parallels in the sage's description of disaster are at times striking, cf. *ANET*[2], pp. 435ff., 445, etc.

[9] Text criticism of 22.1-14: The text is severely disrupted in several places,

2. You boisterous, noisy city, exuberant town!
   Your slain have not been slain with the sword nor are dead in battle,

3. All your rulers have taken to their heels, they have fled far away.
   All of your mighty men have been captured, seized without their bows.

4. Therefore I say: Don't look at me, let me cry bitterly,
   Do not try to comfort me over the destruction of the daughter of my people.

5. For the Lord Yahweh of Hosts has a day of panic, trampling and confusion,
   In the valley of vision was an uproar, noise and shouting against the mountain,

6. Elam took up the quiver. . . .
   And Kir drew from its cover the shield,

7. Your choicest valleys were full of chariots, and horsemen took their stand at the gates.

8. Then he removed the covering of Judah.
   You looked on that day to the weapons in the forest house,

9. And you saw the many breaches of the city of David, and you collected the waters of the lower pool, 10. and you counted the houses of Jerusalem and pulled down the houses to fortify the wall, 11. and you made a reservoir between the two walls for the water of the old pool,
   But you did not look to him who did it, nor pay attention to him who planned it long ago.

12. And Yahweh God of Hosts called in that day
    For weeping and mourning, for baldness and girding with sackcloth,

---

and there is little possibility of reaching a fully satisfactory reconstruction. Cf. the latest attempt of Donner, *Israel unter den Völkern* (Leiden, 1964), pp. 127f. In v. 3 reverse the second part of the lines (3aβ and bβ), and read with the LXX *'ammîṣayikh*. V. 5b is very difficult. M. Weippert's interpretation, *ZAW* 73 (1963), pp. 97ff., has been provisionally adopted. The translation of v. 6aβ is uncertain. To assume, as some do, that it is a corrupt gloss is not much help. 9b-11a seems to be a prose addition which separates the obvious connection between 9a and 11b.

13. But look, frivolity and fun, slaying of beef and slaughtering
    of sheep,
    Eating flesh and drinking wine,
    Eating and drinking: 'Let us eat and drink for tomorrow we
    die!'

14. Yahweh of Hosts has revealed himself in my ears:
    'Surely this shall not be forgiven you until you die.'
    Says Yahweh Lord of Hosts.

Isa. 22.1-14 is one of the most difficult passages in I Isaiah, and
yet in spite of the lack of any consensus it has played a very
important role in fixing the basic attitude of Isaiah toward the
Assyrian crisis. The large number of unsettled problems is
staggering. Is the passage a literary unit? Is the temporal referent
past, future or a combination of different tenses? What is the
form of the oracle? What is the nature of the historical event
which is behind the speech? If one adds to these problems the
present state of the text, then the dimension of the difficulty
becomes clear.

Modern attempts to solve these problems have been largely
dominated by the pioneer work of Duhm.[10] He divided the
passage into two separate oracles, 1-8a and 8b-14, which he thought
were delivered at different times and served different functions.
According to Duhm, the prophet's reaction in the first oracle to
the happy celebration of the people of Jerusalem is motivated by
a sudden vision of impending disaster which overcame him.
Therefore, vv. 2b-7 refer to the future event and the terrors of
the coming siege. Whereas vv. 8b-14 are a proclamation of punishment directed to Jerusalem shortly before an invasion which
criticize the unseemly behaviour and lack of faith in the people.
This interpretation with some slight modification has been
accepted by the majority of modern commentators.[11]

In recent years another interpretation has been defended which
is strikingly different. H. L. Ginsberg[12] suggests that vv. 1-4
represent a later stage of time than vv. 8b-14, and that Jerusalem

[10] B. Duhm, *Das Buch Jesaia* (Göttingen, 1st ed. 1892; quoted from 3rd 1914),
ad loc.
[11] Skinner, Gray, Procksch, Scott, etc.
[12] H. L. Ginsberg, 'Gleanings in First Isaiah', *M. M. Kaplan Jubilee Volume*
(New York, 1953), pp. 251f. Cf. a somewhat similar interpretation by E. J.
Kissane, *The Book of Isaiah* (Dublin, rev. ed. 1960), *ad loc.*

in vv. 1-4 is not making merry, but rather mourning on the housetops. The point of these introductory verses is sarcastic: So gay Jerusalem is finally mourning! Well, she should have wept earlier—on the 'day of panic, trampling and confusion' (v. 5).

In the light of such a variety of interpretation, the need for a form critical analysis is sorely felt. The superscription is secondary and can be disregarded at first. An introductory formula is missing. The oracle begins immediately with a question directed to the protagonist in the second person singular. The tone of the question is that of reproach,[13] which is then followed by a series of declarations which support the implied criticism in v. 3. The initial impression of spontaneous discourse in heated controversy might lead one at first to see within these verses the reflection of a real disputation (*Streitgespräch*) with a group of people. But there are other indications which would cause us hesitation in drawing this conclusion. The opponent of the prophet is neither an individual (Jer. 28) nor a class of people (Isa. 28.7ff.), but the city of Jerusalem which is personified as a woman. This factor would point to a stylization which is foreign to the spontaneous confrontation of the disputation. Again, the self-reference in v. 4: 'Therefore I say' (*'āmartî*) is rhetorical and would have to be omitted if v. 4 were taken as a direct response of someone involved in the controversy.

The attempt of Ginsburg and Kissane to characterize vv. 1-4 as a type of sarcasm or even lament is not convincing because of the style. The lament, which can easily become a taunt, occurs several times in Isaiah (cf. 1.21; 14.5ff., 12ff.; 23.7) and the style is clearly another. The form in 22.1-4 is primarily an invective, but with the characteristic Isaianic alterations. The implied reproach in the question of 1b is expanded and grounded in the indicatives of 2b. and 3. 'You have nothing to be happy about. Just look at what has happened!' In Isa. 1.4ff. it was observed that the reproach moved out of the usual participial clauses to refer to past events.

---

[13] The idiom *mah-lākh* (lit: what to you) is a common interrogative and expresses a genuine concern to discover the source of a difficulty (e.g. Gen. 21.17). It can also occur in the formal setting of the court (II Sam. 14.5). In its expanded form the concomitant action which evoked the interrogative is attached in a *kî* clause. In Judg. 18.23 the formula is part of a disputation and offers a close parallel to Isa. 22.1. I. Lande, *Formelhafte Wendungen der Umgangssprache im Alten Testament* (Leiden, 1949), p. 45, notices the tone of reproach. Ginsberg's attempt to find sarcasm in 22.1 is not confirmed by the parallels. Ps. 114.5 cannot be used as a support for an ironical use.

In 22.2ff. the cause of the reproach has centred entirely in the realm of past action. Again, like 1.4ff., the invective does not issue in a threat, but takes the form of a lament (v. 4).

In v. 5 the invective is again picked up and once more the grounds of the prophetic reproach relate to events in the past.[14] On the day of 'panic, trampling and confusion', when Jerusalem's choicest valleys were overrun, then she looked to her own weapons (v. 8b) and not to her God who had planned it all (v. 11b). Using the catchword 'in that day', the oracle continues with its reproach in v. 12. Instead of the evoked repentance as intended, the siege had called forth only irresponsible revelry. Typical of the invective, the words of the addressee are quoted. Joined to this final reproach comes the final threat, given in the form of an *Auditionsbericht* (report which has been overheard), and directed to the people in the plural: 'Because of this iniquity, you shall die.' The concluding formula marks the end of the divine oracle.

We conclude that the oracle is a unity. Its form is consistent with the Isaianic invective-threat pattern, and it is not to be taken as a vision of the future or as a taunt. For our problem it is significant that the typical form has been fractured by means of a dominant historical reference, to which the oracle is a reaction. At this point, it is essential that the critical methodology be correct. It is a false move to attempt to correlate the text with some historical event and on the basis of this alleged relationship to interpret the text. Equally misleading is the attempt to reconstruct an event which harmonizes with the accounts in II Kings 18-19. Such techniques usually result in supplying the crucial links and in blurring the actual witness of the text which is being examined. Isa. 22 simply does not provide the necessary information which would allow it to be related directly to a known historical event. In spite of this problem, the passage does supply important historical information. It speaks of a siege of Jerusalem, of frantic preparation, of Assyrian auxiliary troops near the city, of the defeat of Jerusalem's troops, of the flight of the rulers, and of a deliverance of some sort.

Without being able to find the larger historical context, the

---

[14] Cf. G. von Rad, 'The Origin of the Concept of the Day of Yahweh', *JSS* 4 (1959), p. 106, for a discussion of the 'day of Yahweh' as an historical event of the past.

main emphasis of the passage can be understood. The prophet
reproaches the people of Jerusalem for failing to comprehend the
meaning of an event which has just happened to them. The
enemy attack belonged to the plan of Yahweh—he took away
Jerusalem's covering—in order to evoke his people to repentance
in a day of judgment. Rather than this reaction, the city looked
to its own strategy (v. 8a) and did not seek help from Yahweh
(v. 11b). The lifting of the siege produced wild rejoicing. Nowhere does the prophet claim that this relief was an act of God,
nor a sign of deliverance connected with Zion's inviolability.
What was commonly held to be a deliverance, the prophet
designates as destruction. Because of this behaviour, the prophet
pronounces the death of the disobedient people. The striking part
of the oracle is the strange dialectic: Isaiah designates the enemy
siege as Yahweh's plan for repentance, and the moment of
deliverance from the attack as the destruction of his people.

3. Isaiah 28.7-13[15]

7. Also these reel with wine and stagger with strong drink;
    The priest and the prophet reel from strong drink; they are
        befuddled from wine,
    They reel from liquor, their vision is blurred, they fumble in
        giving judgment.

8. For all the tables are full of vomit, no place is without a mess.

9. To whom will he teach knowledge, and to whom will he
        explain a message?
    Those who are just weaned from milk, just taken from the
        breasts?

10. For it is *ṣaw lāṣāw, ṣaw lāṣāw, qaw lāqāw, qaw lāqāw*,[16]
    Here a little, there a little;
    That they may go, and fall backward, and be broken, and
        trapped and caught.

The passage shows unmistakable signs of editorial reworking
in which process the redactor has united several independent

---

[15] Text criticism of Isa. 28.7-13: V. 7 read *bappĕlîliyyāh* with *BH*.

[16] For the problem of how to interpret these lines, cf. the latest suggestion
of W. W. Hallo, 'Isaiah 28.9-13 and the Ugaritic Abecedaries', *JBL* 77 (1958),
pp. 324ff. Traditionally commentators have understood the phrase as either a
sarcastic play on the words 'precept' and 'line' or as drunken muttering.

units from different periods and situations into a kerygmatic unity. The original unit probably began with v. 7b. The oracle has passed through a rather complicated oral tradition. Several different voices are heard, but without clear indication by which to identify the speakers. It seems likely that a disputation is reflected between the prophet and the reveling priests and prophets which accounts for the various speakers. In its present form the oracle does not reflect this encounter directly but reveals a perspective which views the incident from a certain distance. The threat in vv. 11b and 13 is phrased in the third person rather than the second. The priests are described in a state of orgy before their words are quoted which appear to mock the prophet. Vv. 7-10, in spite of their form, serve in the total oracle as an invective, and both designate the addressee as well as supply the cause for the reproach.[17] Their words are quoted which are again taken up in a correspondence pattern with the subsequent threat.[18]

The form of the threat is not typical. The common introductory formula of threat is missing, but a closer look at the content provides a possible reason for the alteration. The word of Yahweh which is spoken in judgment is yet to be fulfilled; it will be mediated through the lips of aliens. The parallel in form and content to 30.15 is close. In both instances the response of quiet trust is rejected and the promise is turned into judgment. The redactor parallels this judgment with the threat of destruction directed to the leaders of Samaria which had been fulfilled in the catastrophe of 721. The southern kingdom is following in the footsteps of the northern and will meet with a similar tragic end.

4. Isaiah 28.14-22[19]

14. Hear the word of Yahweh, you scoffers, who rule this people who are in Jerusalem.

15. Because you have said: 'We have made a covenant with death, and with Sheol we have an agreement,

---

[17] Cf. H. W. Wolff, *Das Zitat im Prophetenspruch* (München, 1937), pp. 37f. = *GSAT*, pp. 94f.

[18] Westermann, *Grundformen*, p. 114.

[19] Text criticism of Isa. 28.14-22: V. 15, read with Q and v. 18 *šôṭ* and *ya'bhōr*. Read *ḥāzūth* with v. 18. Cf. the next chapter for treatment of v. 16, but read *yôsēdh*. V. 18, read *wĕthuphar* with *BH*.

The overwhelming scourge, when it passes through, will not
   come upon us,
For we have made lies our refuge, and in falsehood we have
   taken shelter.'

16. Therefore, thus says the Lord Yahweh
    Behold, I am laying in Zion for a foundation a stone,
    A tested stone, a precious corner stone, of a sure foundation;
    'He who believes will not be in haste'.

17. And I will make justice the line, and righteousness the plum-
    met;
    Hail will sweep away the refuge of lies and waters will over-
    whelm the shelter,

18. Then your covenant with death will be annulled,
    And your agreement with Sheol will not stand,
    When the overwhelming scourge passes through you will be
    crushed by it.

19. As often as it passes through it will take you;
    Even though it pass morning by morning, by day and by
    night,
    And it will be sheer terror to understand the message.

20. For the bed is too short to stretch oneself out on
    And the covering too narrow to wrap oneself in it.

21. For Yahweh will rise up as on Mount Perazim,
    He will arouse himself as in the valley of Gibeon;
    To do his deed—strange is his deed!
    To perform his work—strange is his work!

22. And now do not scoff, lest your bonds be tightened,
    For I have heard a decree of destruction, from Yahweh God
    of Hosts upon the whole earth.

   Again there are clear signs of a redactional activity on the
passage, but the change in form and addressee in v. 14 indicates
the beginning of an originally separate oracle. The form retains
the classical features of the invective-threat pattern. There is a call
to attention (v. 14), followed by the direct reference to the
addressee who is then described in participial clauses. The de-

signation of the cause for the subsequent threat precedes its actual pronouncement. In typical fashion the actual words which are quoted constitute the grounds for the reproach and the means for prophetic irony.[20] V. 16 provides the transitional link 'therefore' (*lākhen*) which introduces the messenger formula. Up to this point the pattern is quite normal. Then there appears a remarkable diversion from the traditional form. Instead of a threat, there follows a word of promise, and only in 17b is the threat delivered. How is this unusual form critical observation to be evaluated?

The great majority of commentators regard the verses of promise as integral to the passage. Certainly in terms of form and content they do not give the impression of a gloss or a later expansion. Only Procksch,[21] among the older commentators, considers the promise to be a separate oracle, but his reasons are largely subjective. Several of the more recent commentators have supported Procksch but without much new evidence.[22] We are strongly inclined to agree with Procksch in holding the promise for a secondary redactional element. The following form critical reasons are offered for this decision:

1. The form of the invective-threat is one of the most frequent patterns in the prophets. It retains a remarkable stability from its earliest occurrence to the post-exilic times.[23] There are no clear cut examples in which such an alteration in the usual form as appears here can be shown to belong to the same level of tradition.

2. It is very unusual in the eighth-century prophets and later to find an oracle of promise introduced in the context of a reproach. Isa. 7.10ff. might appear to offer a parallel. Ahaz's words of unbelief call forth a prophetic word which contains a promise of Immanuel as well as a threat to the house of Ahaz. But the

---

[20] Wolff, *Das Zitat*, pp. 61f. = *GSAT*, pp. 83f.

[21] O. Procksch, *Jesaia* I (Leipzig, 1930) *ad loc.*

[22] R. Fey, *Amos und Jesaja* (Neukirchen-Vluyn, 1963), pp. 120f.; S. Hermann, *Die prophetischen Heilserwartungen im Alten Testament* (Stuttgart, 1965), p. 144.

[23] Cf. the general discussion of Wolff, 'Die Begründungen', pp. 1ff.; Westermann, *Grundformen*, pp. 92ff. Several examples of the unbroken form with the quotation forming the reproach are Amos 4.1ff.; 7.16-17; 8.1-4; Micah 3.9. In Jeremiah and Ezekiel the tendency is for the messenger formula to precede both the invective and the threat or to repeat the formula. Cf. Jer. 5.14; 7.13; 25.8; 35.18; Ezek. 5.7; 13.8; 29.9; 36.2. In Kings usually the messenger formula introduces the invective with the stereotyped expression 'because...' (*ya'an*), I Kings 13.21; 14.7; 20.28; etc. Promises are also introduced in this manner, II Kings 10.30.

form of the sign-act is distinct from the invective-threat and is not a real parallel.

3. There is evidence of a literary seam in v. 17b even though the exact history of its textual development is unclear. The threat in vv. 17bff. follows the familiar pattern of correspondence which is matched to the words of v. 15. It has long been observed that the order is disturbed. V. 17b precedes rather than follows v. 18 and anticipates the flood in 18b. It is not clear whether 17b, perhaps in a simpler form, belonged to the oracle of promise and formed the basis for the later expansion in 15b or whether it itself is a secondary prosaic comment, as Donner suggests. At any rate, the present connection between the two parts of the invective-threat form is not smooth and appears to have suffered some disruption.

We shall, therefore, deal with vv. 16-17b as a separate promise oracle in a later chapter. The primary level of tradition witnesses to a threat delivered to the rulers of Jerusalem who have confidence in their own political machinations.[24] The prophet denounces their intrigue and pronounces radical judgment through destruction. The extent of the original threat is difficult to determine precisely. Vv. 20-22 appear to have been an independent oracle, but joined redactionally in such a way as to offer a commentary on the preceding passage. The parable in 23ff. has been given a similar redactional context.

In summary, although a later tradition was aware of a dialectic between judgment on Jerusalem and salvation for Zion, the primary level speaks only on the judgment directed toward those leaders who have abandoned trust in Yahweh and rest in confidence upon political agreements.

5. Isaiah 29.13-14[25]

13. And Yahweh says:
    'Because this people draw near with their mouth
    And with their lips they honour me, although their hearts are
        far from me,
    And their fear of me is a human commandment learned by
        rote,

---

[24] Cf. the commentaries for the various interpretations of the 'covenant with death'.
[25] Text criticism of Isa. 29.13-14: V. 14 read the ptc. with *BH*.

14. Therefore will I again do marvellous things with this people,
    wonderful and marvellous;
    And the wisdom of their wise men shall fail,
    And the prudence of their prudent men shall be hid.,

This passage is very similar in form and content to Isa. 28.14ff. The invective expressed in the motivation clause (*ya°an* = because)[26] precedes and grounds the threat introduced by 'therefore' (*lākhen*) in v. 14. Following the later tendency, both invective and threat are expressed as a divine speech. While there is no sure indication of dating, its redactional place in the book as well as the consistency of the message seem to place it in the late period leading up to the events of 701. The threat is couched in the mysterious terms of the marvellous (*pele'*) which reacts to the lip service of a disobedient people. The plan of Yahweh will invalidate the human advice of the wise counsel and bring forth something totally unexpected.[27] The paradoxical character of God's purpose can bring no comfort to Israel.

6. Isaiah 30.1-5[28]

1. 'Woe to the rebellious children'—oracle of Yahweh—
   'Who carry out a plan, but not mine;
   Who dedicate an alliance, but not of my spirit, adding sin to sin;

2. Who are on the way down to Egypt without asking for my counsel,
   To take refuge in the protection of Pharaoh,
   And to seek shelter in the shadow of Egypt.

3. Therefore the protection of Pharoah shall turn to your shame,
   And the shelter in the shadow of Egypt to your rebuke.

4. For though his officials are at Zoan and his envoys reach Hanes,

5. Everyone comes to shame through a people who cannot profit them,
   That brings neither help nor profit, but shame and disgrace.'

---

[26] Cf. the basic treatment of Wolff, 'Die Begründungen', pp. 5ff. = *GSAT*, pp. 14ff.

[27] J. Fichtner, 'Jahves Plan in der Botschaft des Jesaja', *ZAW* 63 (1951), pp. 16ff.

[28] Text criticism of Isa. 30.1-5: V. 5 read with Q *hōbhîš*.

The passage, in spite of some difficulty in v. 4,[29] falls into the familiar pattern of the invective-threat. Using the form of a divine speech, the woe designates both the addressee and presents the grounds for the polemic. The threat begins in v. 3, followed by a concessive clause. Sufficient parallels of this type are available within the threat to prevent one from supposing a new beginning in v. 3. (cf. Hos. 8.10; Isa. 31.2; Jer. 4.30; 11.11; 22.24; Ezek. 14.14, etc.).

The message sets forth clearly the contrast between Israel's plan for herself and Yahweh's plan. Israel seeks protection as a vassal under the shadow of Egypt and enters into an alliance. She pours out a libation to seal her part! But it is not according to Yahweh's plan. Egypt is unable to help in spite of her apparent power. The outcome will be shame, humiliation, and disgrace.

7. Isaiah 31.1-3[30]

1. Woe to them who go down to Egypt for help, and rely on horses,
   Who trust in chariots because they are many
   And in horsemen because they are very powerful,
   But do not look to the Holy One of Israel or consult Yahweh.

2. Yet he too is wise and brings evil,
   He does not call back his words,
   But will arise against the house of the evil doers,
   And against the helpers of them who work iniquity.

3. The Egyptians are men and not God;
   Their horses are flesh and not spirit.
   When Yahweh stretches out his hand,
   The helper will stumble, and he who is helped will fall,
   And they will all perish together.

This brief passage, with a similar theme as 30.1-5, has usually been considered a simple, straightforward oracle which could be dated with some confidence in the period of the political intrigue with Egypt shortly before 701. Procksch is confident: 'In vv. 1-3 the text and meaning is clear.'[31] Nevertheless in spite of the con-

---

[29] Cf. A. Kuschke, 'Zu Jes. 30,1-5', *ZAW* 64 (1952), pp. 194f. and Donner, *op. cit.*, pp. 132ff.
[30] Text criticism of Isa. 31.1-3: V. 2 read *wĕyābhĭ'* with *BH*.
[31] Procksch, *op. cit.*, p. 404.

sensus regarding its dating, there are problems from the perspective of form criticism which have not been adequately treated.

The oracle begins as a typical invective with the woe exclamation, followed by participial and verbal clauses which designate the offenders and describe the misdeed. The latter is expressed in terms of what they do and fail to do. Up to this point the parallel with 30.1 is clear and the typical pattern of the reproach is followed. Then the problems set in. How is one to understand v. 2? Procksch attempts joining 2a to v. 1, as a concessive clause which modifies Yahweh, and suggests understanding 2b as the beginning of the threat. But 2a and 2b appear to belong together and not to introduce the main threat which first comes in 3b. Moreover, the almost reflective style fits very poorly in an invective. The Septuagint seems to recognize the difficulty and alters the meaning slightly to overcome the difficulty: 'He has wisely brought evils upon them, and his word shall not be frustrated.' This merely avoids the problem. Again, v. 2 anticipates the striking contrast in v. 3 of the Egyptians and God, while repeating in prosaic fashion the comprehensive character of the judgment.

One of the strikingly new features in the passage is the manner in which the contrast is made. Woe is pronounced on those who go to Egypt. They seek help, rely on horses, trust in the multitude of chariots and in the strength of horsemen. They do these things instead of looking to the Holy One of Israel and consulting Yahweh. Then v. 3 returns to the same antithesis of Egypt vs. Yahweh, but this time with a profound theological formulation by means of a proportion. Egypt is to Yahweh as man is to deity, as flesh is to spirit. V. 3 serves in the passage as an elaboration and *précis* of the grounds of the prophetic reproach. The expected threat which then follows picks up and climaxes the two-pronged attack: the helper and the helped will perish together. But this interpretation again illustrates the difficulty of v. 2. The sudden shift away from the contrast of the Egyptians with Yahweh to defend Yahweh's wisdom and power appears to belabour that which is otherwise assumed, namely, the power of Yahweh to bring disaster.

We, therefore, suggest that v. 2 be understood as a subsequent interpolation.[32] Once the initial 'and also' (*wĕgham*) is removed as

---

[32] So also Donner, *op. cit.*, p. 135 for different reasons.

a secondary connective, a clear hymnic couplet appears. Beside the formal reasons, a study of the vocabulary of v. 2 points in this same direction. The stereotyped characterization of the enemy as 'evil doers' (*měrē'îm*) and 'workers of iniquity' (*pō'ălê 'āwen*) is almost entirely confined to the Psalter. This lack of specificity is in striking contrast to v. 3b. The theme of Yahweh's wisdom in contrast to the stupidity of the wicked is also common in the psalms and later prophets (cf. Ps. 94; Jer. 10.6ff.).

Finally, a comparison of Isa. 31.1-3 with 30.1-5 would tend to confirm the theory of interpolation. The close parallel, both in form and content, has often been noticed. Almost each phrase in 30.1-3 has a corresponding member in 31.1-3 with the exception of 31.2 which is without a parallel.

Once v. 2 has been removed, the original form of the oracle emerges with greater clarity. Again the pattern is the invective-threat. The misdeed of seeking help from the military might of Egypt rather than consulting the Holy One of Israel is not only stupid—Egypt is simply flesh and blood—but this calls for the fearful vengeance of Yahweh against both parties involved.

8. Isaiah 30.8-17[33]

8. And now, go write it before them on a tablet, and inscribe it
in a book,
That it may be for a future day, as a testimony for ever.

9. For they are a rebellious people, lying sons,
Children who will not hear the instructions of Yahweh;

10. Who say to the seers, 'See not!'
And to the prophets: 'Prophesy not to us what is right!
Speak to us of pleasant things, prophesy illusions,

11. Leave the way, turn aside from the path,
Let us hear no more of the Holy One of Israel!'

12. Therefore thus says the Holy One of Israel,
'Because you reject this word,
And trust in extortion and deceit and rely on them;

13. Therefore this iniquity shall be to you like a break in a high
wall,

[33] Text criticism of Isa. 30.8-17: V. 8 read *lě'ēdh* with BH.

Bulging out, and about to collapse,
Whose crash comes suddenly, in an instant;

14. And its smashing is like the smashing of a potter's vessel
Which is shattered so completely that among its fragments not
a sherd is found
With which to lift fire from the hearth
Or to dip up water out of the cistern.'

15. For thus says the Lord Yahweh, The Holy One of Israel,
'By conversion and rest you shall be saved;
In quiet and in trust shall be your strength.'
But you would not, 16. and you said,
'No, we will speed upon horses'; therefore, you shall speed
away;
And, 'We will ride upon swift mounts'; therefore, your
pursuers shall be swift!
A thousand shall flee at the threat of one,
At the threat of five you shall flee,

17. Until you are left like a flagpole on the top of a mountain,
Like a signal on a hill.

This powerful oracle, in spite of certain difficulties in interpretation, is clear and straightforward from a form critical perspective. The prophet receives a private oracle to inscribe a message in a book (8b). This message is to serve as a witness to a later generation because the present one has rejected the prophet's preaching. The motivation for the private instruction is given in a form closely resembling the invective in which the words of the rebellious, addressed in the third person, are quoted as grounds against them (vv. 9-11).

Then there follows two examples of the invective-threat pattern, which although once independent units, now serve to illustrate the message which is to be preserved for the future. The return to the second person contrasts with the style of v. 9. In both instances the reproach precedes the threat. The prophetic message of quiet trust has been rejected. In the second oracle the quotation of the words of promise along with the words of rejection heighten the effect of the judgment (15ff.). The words are a summary of the Isaianic message: deliverance comes in calm dependence on Yahweh who has committed himself to this people. By rejecting this avenue of hope, disobedient Israel calls down upon itself radical disaster. It is difficult to imagine how a more absolute and final message of judgment could be pictured. One is reminded of Amos in the stark, unmitigated oracle of divine threat.

To summarize: The form of the invective-threat shows strong affinities to the classical patterns of oral discourse which appear in Amos. However, there are certain characteristic differences. Introductory formulae are often missing (1.4; 22.1; 28.7), and concluding ones are infrequent (22.14). The invective is still distinguishable from the threat which follows, and often makes use of the transitional adverb (30.3, 13). While occasionally the invective is a prophetic speech, usually it consists of Yahweh's words along with the threat (29.13; 30.1, 18). The close connection between invective and threat also tends to loosen. In 1.4ff. the invective concludes in a lament while in 22.12ff. and 28.11ff. the threat arises out of a disputation which serves as an invective. The oracles in 30.12ff. show signs of redactional ordering while secondary interpolations seem likely in 28.16 and 31.2.

In terms of the content, a clear picture emerges. The words of reproach and judgment are directed to the leaders of Jerusalem who are engaged in planning government policy (28.14; 30.1; 31.1), or appear associated with a militant anti-Assyrian party (28.7). Nevertheless, the entire people participate in the folly (1.4f.; 22.1), and share the ensuing misery. Although the weight of the blame falls on the leaders, there appears no principle restriction or limitation respecting the judgment, neither temporal, nor ethical, nor geographical. The invective, in contrast to Amos, centres in Israel's attempt to find security and refuge through political strategy rather than by sole trust in Yahweh. They make their own plans (30.1), but fail to discern the purpose of Yahweh (22.12). The ethical criticism is still present, but it is subsumed under the major category of disbelief. The promises of deliverance, because they are rejected, are turned to judgment (30.15ff.); in fact, the present evil generation is abandoned in its hardening (30.8ff.). The instrument of judgment is described in various ways (28.17; 30.13-17), but Assyria is clearly in mind (28.11). The emphasis on unconditional, radical judgment is not softened by a theory of a remnant, sacred city, or pedagogical chastisement. It belongs to the plan of Yahweh which is characterized by its strange, unexpected, and terrifying quality (28.21; 29.14). There is no indication that the invective-threat was confined to one period or that it was ever abandoned or seriously altered during Isaiah's ministry.

B. THE ORACLES AGAINST THE NATIONS

1. Isaiah 14.24-27[34]

24. Yahweh of Hosts has sworn, saying:
    'As I have planned, so shall it be,
    And as I have purposed, so shall it happen,

25. That I will break Assyria in my land
    And will tread him down on my mountains.
    Then his yoke shall depart from them
    And his burden shall leave their shoulders.'

26. This is the plan which is formed concerning the whole earth;
    And this is the hand which is stretched out against the nations.

27. For Yahweh of Hosts has formed a plan, and who can frustrate it?
    And his hand is stretched out, and who can turn it back?

The majority of commentators agree that the passage appears incomplete. The most frequent suggestion, which has been defended in the past especially by Cheyne and Procksch, has been to join this passage with the invective in 10.5-15. However, from a form critical perspective, this suggestion hardly recommends itself. As it now stands, the unit begins with a threat which is introduced by a swear formula. The introduction of a threat by means of an oath is not uncommon in the prophets (Amos 4.2; 6.8; etc.), and in II Isaiah an oath can also introduce a promise (54.9; 61.8). In v. 25b a latent promise also appears.

An examination of the oath formula indicates a wide range of possible formulations. Usually the introductory formula is in the third person singular as is the case here, but it can also be given in the first person (Jer. 22.5; 49.13). The agent of actual threat can be Yahweh speaking in the first person (Amos 6.8; 8.7) or with

---

[34] Text criticism of Isa. 14.24-27: V. 24, 1QIsaᵃ reads *thyh* instead of *hyth* which provides a better parallelism but is not necessary grammatically.

Yahweh as the subject of indirect address (Amos 4.2f.). More significant is that the threat is at times addressed directly to its recipient (Amos 4.2; Jer. 5.14), while at other times the threat belongs to the self-counsel of Yahweh (Amos 6.8). In Isa. 14.24 Yahweh does not address Assyria directly, nor is the form that of a monologue (Procksch). Rather, two parallel passages in Isaiah (5.9; 22.14) would suggest the form of a decision which was over-heard by the prophet—an *Auditionsbericht*.

In vv. 26ff. the prophet takes up the word in the form of the 'summary-appraisal'.[35] The content of the form is of fundamental importance for Isaiah's attitude toward Assyria. There is no hint that the prophet has changed his mind concerning Assyria's role, nor is it really possible to assign a specific date to the oracle without a preconceived theory of the prophet's development. Isaiah emphasizes rather that Yahweh's decision to destroy Assyria rests on a total plan which includes all the nations. The picture is of Yahweh as a mighty warrior trampling on the body of prostrate Assyria. The oracle speaks of Yahweh's shattering Assyria 'in my land . . . upon my mountains', which establishes the setting for the defeat. However, this formulation does not point to any specific features of the Zion tradition; in fact, the plural 'mountains' is not the common expression within the traditional vocabulary. The emphasis on the purpose of Yahweh has given a close unity to the passage. It is also significant that the theme of Assyria's destruction is introduced as a threat, and is not directed to Jerusalem as words of comfort. While one could argue that logically any threat against Assyria was an indirect comfort to Israel, the study of traditions should distinguish between a possible deduction and oracles of direct consolation which use the theme of Assyria such as 10.24ff.

2. Isaiah 10.5-15[36]

5. Woe, Assyria, rod of my anger, staff () of my fury.

---

[35] Cf. Excursus I.

[36] Text criticism of Isa. 10.5-15: V. 5, H. L. Ginsberg, *JBL* 69 (1950), p. 54, suggests reading the mem in *bhĕyādhām* as an eclitic mem and so retaining the MT. However, the resulting expression 'in the hand of my wrath' is odd and without a biblical parallel. Also it destroys the obvious parallelism in the text. Therefore, eliminate the phrase *hû'bhĕyādhām* as a gloss. For a critical appraisal of the whole problem of the enclitic mem in the O.T., see the recent unpublished Yale dissertation of David A. Robertson, *Linguistic Evidence in Dating Early Hebrew Poetry* (1966). V. 12, *BH* follows the LXX in

6. Against a godless nation I send him, and against the people of
   my wrath I charge him,
   To spoil and to plunder and to trample them down like the
   mud of the streets.

7. But not so does he think, and not so does he plan;
   Rather it is in his heart to destroy and to cut off not a few
   nations;

8. For he says: Are not my commanders all kings?

9. Is not Calno like Carchemish?
   Is not Hamath like Arpad? Is not Samaria like Damascus?

10. As my hand has found the kingdoms of the idols
    Whose graven images were greater than those of Jerusalem
    and Samaria,

11. Shall I not do to Jerusalem and her idols
    As I have done to Samaria and her images?

12. And it shall come to pass when Yahweh has finished all his
    work on Jerusalem, I will punish the arrogant boasting of
    the king of Assyria and his haughty pride. 13. For he says:
    By the strength of my hand I have done it,
    And by my wisdom, for I have understanding;
    I have taken away the boundaries of peoples,
    And have plundered their treasures;
    And like a mighty one I laid low the inhabitants.

14. My hand has seized the wealth of the peoples like a nest,
    And as men gather eggs that have been forsaken,
    So have I gathered all the earth.
    And there was none that moved a wing,
    Nor opened the mouth, nor peeped.

15. Shall the axe vaunt itself over him who hews with it,
    Or the saw magnify itself against him who wields it?
    As if a stick should wield him who lifts it,
    Or as if a staff should lift him who is not wood!

The scope of this extremely difficult passage is not easy to

---

suggesting that the verb be emended to the third person. Cf. the discussion
in the chapter for retaining the MT. V. 13, read the two verbs with waw
consecutives as in v. 14. V. 13b is very corrupt, but the many suggested
emendations remain highly conjectural (cf. especially Duhm).

determine. There are many signs that the original oracle has undergone subsequent expansion. Yet this possibility cannot be used as an invitation for wholesale neglect of the present inner structure of the passage.[37] The initial *hôy* (woe) in v. 5 forms now a secondary catchword connection with the preceding oracle, but serves an integral function within the oracle which is independent of this secondary connection. V. 16 introduces a threat against Assyria which was clearly understood by the redactor as resulting from his haughty speech of arrogance. The majority of modern commentators are inclined to see this threat as a secondary expansion of the original oracle, and in this judgment we concur.[38]

If the unit is narrowed to vv. 5-15, what can now be said about its form? The passage is constructed out of a variety of smaller oracles which have been linked together in a number of ways. Vv. 5-7 is a woe oracle directed against Assyria in the form of a Yahweh speech. Vv. 8-11 presents the first speech of Assyria which is characterized by its dominant interrogative style. V. 12 is a prose sentence which comments on the second speech of Assyria, an oracle of self-praise in vv. 13-14. Finally, v. 15 is a wisdom saying which has the form of a disputation fable.

Most modern commentators seek to eliminate the prose sentence of v. 12 immediately as a secondary gloss. Certainly in its present form it raises problems. The verse interrupts the first person speech of Assyria, and bluntly describes Assyria's judgment within a chronological order which reflects a typically later pattern. Commentators have, therefore, frequently attempted to eliminate v. 12 and to join all or part of the first speech of Assyria (vv. 8-11) with vv. 13-14 (so Duhm and Donner). The result is to simplify a complexity of oracles into one consistent, first person speech of Assyria. However, this movement destroys the essential structure of the present oracle and is, therefore, not advisable. It is essential that the two Assyrian speeches he retained as separate units. As we shall see, the oracles are distinct both in terms of form and content.

The oracle opens with a woe particle directed against Assyria, and not just a simple exclamation as is sometimes the case (17.12;

---

[37] Cf. K. Fullerton, 'The Problem of Isaiah, Chapter 10', *AJSL* 34 (1918), pp. 170ff. for an example of a brilliant interpretation which does just this.
[38] Cf. O. Kaiser, *Der Prophet Jesaja*[2] (Göttingen, 1963), for a good summary of the reasons.

18.1; Jer. 30.7; 47.6). The Yahweh speech follows generally the form of an invective. Assyria does not intend to follow Yahweh's plan, and, typical for the invective is the use of his own words to document this misdeed. It is important to observe the connection between the invective of Yahweh and the Assyrian speech. The charge is made in v. 7 that Assyria intends to 'cut off not a few nations'. This is then illustrated in the Assyrian speech which follows. The essential point of the speech is the intention to lay claim on Jerusalem in a similar manner as was done with the other cities. The oracle takes on even greater focus if the 'godless nation' of v. 6 is understood as Samaria. The play on words in v. 6b and 8.1 would suggest this interpretation. The historical setting of the oracle is then narrowed to the period just before Assyria turns its forces on Jerusalem.

However, there remain certain problems in vv. 10-11 connected with Assyria's first speech. Both the syntax and the content of v. 10 is difficult to interpret. The whole line is grammatically an anacoluthon which also breaks the interrogative style of 9 and 11. Moreover, the verse contrasts Jerusalem and Samaria with the rest of the kingdoms, while in the next verse Jerusalem is set over against Samaria. For these reasons we hold v. 10 for a secondary interpolation. V. 11 then emerges clearly as the major focus of the speech.

Still there is a difficulty with the present form of v.11. The issue at stake is Assyria's arrogance in disregarding the limits set for her in the prior plan of Yahweh. The claim is made that no nation, either in the past or the future, can oppose her armies. But this major point is confused by another theme in v. 11. Yahweh is placed in the same category with the empty idols: 'shall I not do to Jerusalem and her idols as I have done to Samaria and to her images?' The issue is now one of blasphemy, and not just of arrogant disobedience. Kaiser[39] even suggests that this verse has introduced a new note from which the prophetic legend in II Kings 19.10-13 = Isa. 37.10-13 has sprung. This note of blasphemy does not appear elsewhere in the primary poetic oracles of Isaiah. It seems much more probable to understand this motif as a secondary development which intensified Assyria's grievance by moving it from disobedience to blasphemy.[40] If the two words 'her idols'

[39] Kaiser, _op. cit._, _ad loc._
[40] Cf. below for a further treatment of this motif.

(wĕlĕ' ĕlîlêhā) and 'her images' (wĕla'ăṣabbēhā) are removed, then a bicolon consistent with the rest of the oracle is restored. At the same time the one charge of flaunting the plan of Yahweh now emerges with great clarity.

The suggestion has been made that the first Assyrian speech serves to illustrate the charge being made by Yahweh in v. 7. The second Assyrian speech follows this same structural pattern. In v. 12 Yahweh's purpose 'to punish the arrogant boasting of the king of Assyria' is asserted. What follows is a speech of pure self-praise which has been achieved by caricaturing the ancient Near Eastern inscriptional style with its endless lists of past victories in the boastful repetition of the first person: 'I have done it . . . I have removed . . . I have gathered. . . .' The indicative style in the past tense sets it apart formally from the interrogative style with its reference to the future which characterizes the first speech. V. 12 does not function in the passage as a gloss which simply disrupts the single Assyrian speech. Rather, it plays a role parallel to v. 7 in presenting the issue which is then illustrated by the speech which follows. However, in its present form the verse has certainly been expanded, which has resulted in some of the problems noted above. One suggestion would be to remove the temporal clause in 12a as a gloss. This may have entered when interest focused on specifying the sequence of the judgment. Then the first person speech of the Massoretic Text can be retained in a poetic line which is consistent with 5ff.: 'Surely (kî) I will punish the arrogant boasting of the king of Assyria and his haughty pride.'

The oracle concludes with a wisdom saying which succeeds in making its critical point effectively as well as adding a note of prophetic sarcasm. The prophet, not Yahweh, is the speaker and the verse summarizes his criticism for the entire oracle. The closest parallel appears in 29.15ff. which also introduces a wisdom saying by means of a woe oracle (cf. Isa. 45.9ff.; Rom. 9.20ff.). Gressmann noted the element of the disputation in this wisdom form.[41] In the light of his analysis, and the other elements of disputation in vv. 8-11 which Begrich pointed out,[42] one might

---

[41] H. Gressmann, *Israels Spruchweisheit* (Berlin, 1925), pp. 28f. On the question of the forms of the fable, cf. W. Richter, *Traditionsgeschichtliche Untersuchungen zum Richterbuch* (Bonn, 1963), pp. 282ff.

[42] J. Begrich, *Studien zu Deuterojesaja* (repr. München, 1963), pp. 48f.

wonder whether the whole unit was in fact patterned after the form of the disputation. While the theory remains attractive, it cannot be sustained form critically. The decisive objection is that the Assyrian speeches in relation to the Yahweh speeches do not function as claim and counter-claim which clash in confrontation. There is no direct encounter as in Isa. 28.7ff. Rather, the Assyrian claim appears each time bracketted within a Yahweh oracle and serves as grounds for the judgment. The form of the oracle is the invective-threat and the non-typical elements bear the strong stamp of Isaiah's own literary creativity. The prophet has employed a form, which was traditionally directed against social abuses, and redirected it to the political realities of his day. The invective form may have effected the use of the frequentative tense (v. 6), but in general the area of the misdeed has been shifted to historical occurrences (v. 9).

What seems clear from this analysis is that the theological understanding of Yahweh's plan has been the leading force in shaping the traditional material. There is no indication in the text that a rationale is being offered to explain a shift in the perspective of the prophet. The oracle does not focus on Isaiah's role as prophet. Rather, the oracle asserts the clear conflict between Yahweh's plan and Assyria's intention. The oracle does not serve as a disputation between opposing parties. The clever use of the wisdom saying sets a different tone. The effect is produced of a calm—almost distant—evaluation of a situation with a reflective confidence as to the certain outcome.

3. Isaiah 18.1-6

1. Ah! land of whirring wings, which lies beyond the rivers of
   Ethiopia;

2. That sends envoys by sea in vessels of papyrus upon the waters.
   Go, you swift messengers, to a nation, tall and sleek,
   To a people feared near and far,
   To a nation mighty and triumphant whose land rivers divide.

3. All you inhabitants of the world, you dwellers on the earth,
   When a signal is raised on the mountains, look!
   When a trumpet is blown, listen!

4. For thus says Yahweh to me:
   'I will look on quietly from my abode,

Like the shimmering heat in sunshine,
Like a cloud of dew in the heat of harvest.'

5. For before the harvest, when the blossom is over
And the berry has become a ripening grape,
He will lop off the branches with pruning hooks
And the tendrils, he will cut away.

6. They shall be left completely to the vultures of the mountains
and the beasts of the earth.
And the vultures will summer upon them,
And all the beasts of the earth will winter upon them.

This oracle is one of the most perplexing in the whole Isaianic collection. It is filled with lexicographical and form critical problems which continue to resist a clear interpretation. It is not at all obvious why the prophet should describe to the messengers a people to which they themselves belong. Where is there mention of an explicit rejection of an alliance? And why is the term 'go' used, if the messengers are to return to Ethiopia? There is no indication in the text that v. 3 contains a message which the envoys are to take. The change in the subject to 'all you inhabitants of the world' does not lend itself as a message to Ethiopia. Yet v. 3 with its temporal clause can hardly open a separate oracle and seems to be without parallel in Isaiah with this function. Nevertheless, the similarity in content with 14.26, which is a message to the whole world, is far too impressive to allow one to remove it as a later interpolation.

In spite of this failure to understand the text as a whole, a few observations can be made regarding the content. A private oracle to Isaiah communicates a picture of Yahweh's unruffled self-composure which arises from his sense of absolute sovereignty over the whole world. But at the given moment, as certain as the harvest, he will cut away the branches and prune the tree. In the context, the threat is directed toward Assyria whose army will be left dead to the scavengers of the field. It is possible that the vocabulary reflects some slight influence from the Zion tradition, particularly in v. 4 (cf. Pss. 97.2; 104.5). However, this is fully subordinate to the theology of Yahweh's plan for the destruction of the enemy.

In this connection, it may be in order to mention briefly the

earlier oracle in 8.9-10,[43] which offers a parallel in the manner by
which the theology of Yahweh's plan has made use of the Zion
tradition. The passage is generally assigned, with good reasons,
to the period of the Syrian-Ephramaic war. In this word directed
against the nations the prophet pronounces with confidence the
frustration of their plans, and sets over against them the fact of
Yahweh's presence: 'God is with us.' This familiar vocabulary of
the Zion tradition[44] makes it clear that the prophet has not
retreated suddenly into a quietistic meditation, but that he is con-
firming by means of this catchword from the tradition Yahweh's
present role as absolute sovereign. The intrigues and machinations of the enemy—whether the coalition, Assyria, or whoever—
will be smashed by the God of Zion. While it is evident from this
passage that the plan of Yahweh does not appear in the fully
developed form of the later period, in its basic thrust the affirma-
tion is the same as in the later crisis.

4. Isaiah 30.27-33[45]

27. Behold, the name of Yahweh comes from far, burning is his
    anger and heavy the rising smoke,
    His lips are full of fury and his tongue is like a devouring fire;

28. His breath is like a sweeping torrent that reaches up to the
    neck,
    To sift the nations with the sieve of destruction
    And to place on the jaws of the peoples a bridle which leads to
    ruin.

29. But for you there will be a song as in the night when a feast is
    held,
    And joy of heart as when one sets out to the sound of flute to
    go to the house of Yahweh, to the rock of Israel.

[43] Cf. M. Saebø, 'Zur Traditionsgeschichte von Jesaia 8, 9-10', *ZAW* 76
(1964), pp. 132ff.

[44] The phrase 'Yahweh with us' also appears in other ancient traditions
outside of the Zion circle. Cf. Num. 14.43; Judg. 6.13.

[45] Text criticism of Isa. 30.27-33: V. 27, *wĕkhōbhedh maśśā'āh* is an old crux.
Is the *hapax* to be interpreted as 'rising smoke' or 'exultation'? In the context
the former seems preferable. V. 29b is surely overloaded. V. 32, read with
many mss. *mûsārāh*. The text of 32b and 33 appears to have suffered severe
corruption with little chance of restoration possible. The versions vary
greatly. cf. Gressmann and Procksch for suggested emendations.

30. And Yahweh will cause his majestic voice to be heard and the
    descent of his arm to be seen,
    In a frenzy of anger, and a flame of consuming fire, with a
    cloudburst and rain storm and hail.

31. The Assyrians will be dismayed by the voice of Yahweh when
    he smites with a rod.

32. And every stroke of the rod of punishment which Yahweh
    shall lay upon them will be to the sound of timbrels and
    lyres as he attacks them with brandished arm.

33. For a pyre has long been prepared, even for the king it is
    made ready,
    Its fire-pit is deep and wide with fire and wood in abundance,
    The breath of Yahweh, like a stream of brimstone, kindles it.

This grandiose oracle raises a whole battery of form critical and
traditio-critical problems, many of which have long been seen, but
hardly solved. In the first place, how is the form of the oracle to
be characterized? There are no introductory or concluding
formulae to aid in the analysis. At first glance vv. 27-28 appear
as part of a theophanic hymn to Yahweh's power, but seen within
its larger context, especially vv. 30ff., the element of prophetic
threat becomes clear. The traditional sequence of the uproar of
the natural elements has now been replaced by the panic of the
nations. This is a threat for the future against Assyria, which
belongs to the larger pattern of the oracle against the nations.
Along with this, and embedded within the oracle, is another
element. In v. 29 Israel is addressed in the second person with a
word of promise. The destruction of Assyria does not just evoke
joy as in a festival, but actually is set within a festival itself. Israel
will be singing songs of praise while Assyria's punishment will be
accompanied by timbrels and lyres. Indeed, the form of the
destruction is pictured as a gigantic sacrifice and Yahweh as a
type of Molèch who kindles the pyre with his breath.[46]
    This combination in one oracle of a threat against Assyria and
a promise to Israel raises a difficult form critical problem. How is
one to explain its occurrence together in the light of the fact that
nowhere else in the primary oracles of Isaiah are these two forms
so combined? This is not to say that the motifs of judgment of

[46] H. Gressmann, *Der Messias* (Göttingen, 1929), pp. 111ff.

the nations and salvation for Israel do not appear. Rather, the issue is that the literary forms of the threat and the promise are not otherwise combined in this manner. In Isa. 14.24f. the threat against Assyria includes an implication of salvation for Israel, but not in an oracle of promise which is addressed to Israel. The same is true in 10.5ff.; 17.12ff.; and 29.5ff. It is only in the obviously secondary oracles in I Isaiah that the combination is made. Thus, for example, in 10.24ff.; 26.20ff.; 30.23ff., a threat against the nations is fused with a promise oracle to Israel. Moreover, the method in which the combination has been executed in these secondary passages is important. The oracle usually begins with the promise to Israel and concludes with the threat to the nations. The promise oracle has almost entirely subordinated the threat. The latter is no longer an independent element, such as an oracle against the nations, but merely an illustrative element within the promise. This promise pattern is characteristic of post-exilic literature.

Now the form critical problem of 30.27ff. emerges with more clarity. On the one hand, 30.27ff. evidences a combination of oracles, combining elements of threat and promise, which is unusual for I Isaiah. On the other hand, the independent and original character of the threat is not at all paralleled in the later tradition in which the promise element is pre-eminent. This condition would seem to indicate that from a form critical point of view there is little justification for regarding the oracle as secondary and assigning it to the post-exilic period (*contra* Marti, Donner). A more probable solution would be to recognize as primary tradition the threat oracle which was directed against Assyria by Isaiah. Subsequently elements from a promise oracle were added in vv. 29 and 32 (so Scott). This solution has more to commend it than the rearrangement of verses suggested by Procksch.

There is another way to approach the material which can serve as a check on the form critical analysis, namely, through a study of the history of traditions. It has long been recognized that Isa. 30.27ff. reflects traditional material of the theophany of Yahweh which is paralleled in the early hymns. The recent study of J. Jeremias[47] has focused on clarifying the formal structures of this tradition, and on delineating a form critical development. He

[47] J. Jeremias, *Theophanie* (Neukirchen-Vluyn, 1965), pp. 56ff.

reconstructs an original form which possessed two parts. The
first described the coming of Yahweh, the second the uproar in
nature caused by his arrival. In the development of the form the
individual parts were either expanded, or separated from one
another and developed independently. This analysis has much to
commend it. Jeremias also attempts to find an original setting for
this form and finally decides on the victory song of the holy war.
This part of the analysis appears much less convincing. In fact,
the difficulty which the author encounters and the improbability
of his solution, raises the question of whether one can really speak
of a 'theophany form'. It would seem more likely that there is a
theophany tradition which very early accommodated itself to
different forms. Just as one cannot speak meaningfully of an
Exodus form or a Sinai form, so also here, we are dealing with
traditional material rather than one literary form. The decisive
difference would be that the tradition of Yahweh's theophany at
an early stage found the hymn to be its most natural form which
would account for the stereotyped pattern in which the material
usually appears.

It is of interest to note the variety of forms in which the tradition of the theophany occurs. In the Psalms the tradition appears
within a hymn (Pss. 68; 29; Judg. 5), a thanksgiving psalm
(Ps. 18), a complaint (Ps. 77), and a cult liturgy (Ps. 50). Again, in
the prophetic oracles the use of the tradition shows tremendous
variety. It can retain its form as a hymn (Nahum 1) or appear with
new eschatological elements added to it (Hab. 3). It can form the
basis for the prophet proclamation of threat (Amos 1; Micah 1)
or be part of an oracle of judgment against the nations (Jer. 25.30f.).
Finally, the theophanic tradition can be employed as a word of
promise with the threat of destruction directed against Israel's
enemies (cf. Joel 4.16; Ezek. 38.18ff.).

This latter use is of particular interest for our immediate
problem. The great majority of the cases in which the tradition of
the theophany appears in words of promise stem from the post-
exilic period. There are hymns of an early age in which the element
of theophanic judgment on the nations and salvation for Israel
appears, but this is to be distinguished from the use of the theophanic tradition within the form of promise. It is characteristic of
these forms that the appearance of Yahweh in judgment on the
nations is for the benefit of Israel and serves to evoke joy and

comfort in her (cf. Isa. 26.20; 33.3-6; Zech. 9.14; 14.3; Isa. 66.10-16; Ass. Moses 10.5ff.). In other words, a study of the history of theophanic tradition confirms the form critical conclusion in questioning the present combination of traditional elements as belonging to the primary level of Isaianic oracles. Moreover, a study of the other traditions which later became associated with the theophany indicates a similar pattern. The enemy-from-the-north (Ezek. 38f.), the divine warrior (Isa. 40.10; 63.1ff.), and the day of Yahweh (Zech. 14.1; Joel 4.14) all tend to become part of the post-exilic promise oracles, a function which was not originally the case.

To summarize: Our study has indicated that in the primary level of tradition the prophet has employed the ancient tradition of Yahweh's coming in judgment as a threat to Assyria. The oracle is directed to Assyria and the prophet's emphasis is on the majestic power and terrifying might of God in shattering Assyrian power. Yahweh is the source of real terror and furious battle anger. Only at a later date as the focus changed does this threat become joined with an explicit word of promise to Israel.

5. Isaiah 17.12-14

12. Ah, the thunder of many peoples, they thunder like the thunder of the sea.
    And the roaring of nations, that roar like the roaring of mighty waters.

13. The nations roar like the roaring of many waters, but he will rebuke them, and they will flee far away,
    Chased like chaff on the mountains before the wind and whirling dust before the storm.

14. At evening time, behold, terror! Before morning, they are no more!
    This is the portion of them who despoil us, and the lot of them who plunder us.

It has long been recognized that this passage makes use of ancient tradition. The unnamed enemy which roars down upon Israel in attack is pictured in the vocabulary of the chaotic waters of the cosmic deep which threaten to engulf the people of God. Suddenly, Yahweh intervenes and miraculously the danger is passed. The stereotyped expressions—the 'roaring of the sea', the 'mighty waters', 'he rebukes', 'before morning', 'they are no more'—confirm the judgment that this material is akin to the Zion tradition of the psalms (cf. Pss. 46; 48; 76). Moreover, recent research[48] has made abundantly clear the provenance and characteristic elements of this tradition.

Now an important question is raised by the newer traditio-critical approach in regard to the particular use of the Zion tradition by the prophet Isaiah. Indeed, one of the crucial questions in the study of Isaiah's relation to Assyria is to determine how he used the Zion tradition. Here the opinions diverge radically. The older literary critics tended to relate the Zion tradition directly to Sennacherib's invasion of 701. The more conservative critics understood the language of the tradition to reflect the historical invasion, and therefore attributed such passages to Isaiah.[49] The more liberal critics interpreted the Zion tradition as a later reflection on Jerusalem's narrow escape and assigned all such references to the post-exilic period.[50] In recent years, the recognition that the Zion tradition is very ancient and its origin independent of the Assyrian invasion has ruled out these direct relationships.[51] The complexity of the problem has now been more clearly seen, but the basic issue has remained unsolved. Did Isaiah himself make use of the Zion tradition, and if so, in what manner? Or was it a secondary level of tradition, reflecting on Isaianic tradition and the events of 701, which reworked his message according to the ancient patterns of the tradition? Before

[48] H. Schmid, 'Jahwe und die Kulttraditionen von Jerusalem', *ZAW* 67 (1955), pp. 168ff.; E. Rohland, *Die Bedeutung der Erwählungstraditionen Israels für die Eschatologie der alttestamentlichen Propheten* (Diss. Heidelberg, 1956), pp. 119ff.; G. von Rad, *Old Testament Theology*, II, (Edinburgh and London, 1965), pp. 155ff.; J. Schreiner, *Sion-Jerusalem Jahwes Königssitz* (München, 1963), pp. 217ff.; E. Lipiński, *La Royaulté de Yahvé dans la Poésie et le Culte de l'Ancien Israël* (Brussel, 1965), pp. 432ff. Most recently G. Wanke, *Die Zionstheologie der Korachiten* (Berlin, 1966), pp. 70ff., has contested the early connection of the chaos motif with the *Völkerkampf* motif. He assigns Pss. 46 and 48 to the post-exilic period because they show a fusion of both motifs. I do not regard his analysis of these traditions as correct. Cf. B. S. Childs, *JBL* 78 (1959), pp. 187ff.

[49] So, for example, Dillmann, *Der Prophet Jesaia* (Leipzig, 1890), *ad loc.*, and more recently, John Bright, *Peake's Commentary on the Bible*, p. 514.

[50] B. Stade, 'Miscellen: Anmerkungen zu 2 Kö. 15-21', *ZAW* 6 (1886), pp. 16f.

[51] Cf. John Hayes, 'The tradition of Zion's Inviolability', *JBL* 82 (1963), pp. 419ff.

we attempt to offer a solution to these questions, it will be
necessary to finish our examination of the Zion passages in Isaiah.
Only when the detailed work has been done can one deal adequately with the larger question.

The form of the oracle in 17.12-14 is not easy to determine. The
earlier attempts to join the oracle either with what preceded or
with what followed does not recommend itself. Some critics[52]
have suggested seeing in the oracle a vision of the prophet who
perceived with the prophet's ear the attacking hordes, but the
characteristic signs for a vision are missing and must be supplied
(cf. Isa. 6.1ff.; Jer. 4.23ff.; Amos 7.1ff.). The watchman's cry
offers a closer parallel (Jer. 4.5f., 4.13) with the excited announce-
ment of impending peril, but the eschatological elements of the
prophetic oracle diverge sharply from this pattern and indicate a
high degree of originality in terms of form. The final line is a
good example of what we have designated as a summary-appraisal form.[53] The prophet, acting after the manner of a wise
man, summarizes his point by generalizing his conclusions into a
broader illustration of a principle. If this observation is correct,
it adds to the evidence that the prophet himself is making use of
the Zion tradition.

The pattern of this tradition emerges with great clarity in the
oracle. A mighty horde, boisterous as the noisy sea, is attacking.
Reference to Jerusalem as the object of the attack is missing, but
it is implied in the tradition. No reason is given for the invasion.
The raging of the nations seems to be a historicized form of the
roar of the chaotic waters against the abode of Yahweh.[54] As
Yahweh once rebuked the sea (Nahum 1.4; Ps. 46.7), now he
rebukes the threatening nations. Then suddenly, before the
morning,[55] the tide turns. Miraculously the danger is passed and
the threat has evaporated. Jerusalem plays completely a passive
role in the deliverance. The prophet adds his appraisal: the
deliverance is not an accident, but will repeat itself according to a
predetermined scheme of judgment on Israel's enemies.

The real function of the oracle is somewhat difficult to assess.

[52] H. Schmidt, *SAT* II/2² (Göttingen, 1923), *ad loc.*
[53] Cf. Excursus I.
[54] Gunkel, *Schöpfung und Chaos* (Göttingen, 1895), pp. 100f. was the first to
have described the tradition with precision.
[55] J. Ziegler, 'Die Hilfe Gottes ,,am Morgen" ', *Alttestamentliche Studien
Friedrich Nötscher* (Bonn, 1950), pp. 281ff.

The form is not that of a direct threat against Assyria. The enemy remains vague and undefined, yet an indirect threat is clearly intended. Nor is the style of the oracle that of a word of comfort to Israel, although again indirectly such may be included. Certainly the role of Jerusalem as a sacred place is greatly de-emphasized. Moreover, there is a surprising reticence in using the name of Yahweh. This stands in sharp contrast to a passage such as 14.24ff. in which the emphasis falls on Yahweh's purpose in smashing the enemy. As a result, the contours of the oracle remain somewhat blurred. The fearful terror of the thundering army vanishes before the eery mystery of a sudden and total deliverance. The effect of the oracle is to highlight this strange side of Yahweh's work before whom the terrors of demonic nations evaporate into thin air.

6. Isaiah 29.1-8[56]

1. Woe Ariel, Ariel, the city against which David encamped,
   Add year to year; let the feasts go around.

2. Then I will distress Ariel, and there shall be mourning and moaning;
   And thou shall be to me like Ariel.

3. And I will encamp against you round about
   And besiege you with towers, and raise siegeworks against you.

4. Then low from the ground you shall speak,
   And deep from the dust your words shall come,
   And like a spirit your voice shall come from the earth
   And your speech shall whisper out of the dust.

5. And the horde of your enemies shall be like fine dust,
   And the horde of the ruthless like passing chaff.
   Then it shall be that in an instant, suddenly,

6. You will be visited by Yahweh of Host
   With thunder and earthquake and great noise,
   With storm and tempest, and the flame of devouring fire.

---

[56] Text criticism of Isa. 29.1-8: V. 3, LXX reads 'like David' (= *kĕdhāwidh*) which may be correct. V. 5, *zryk* often emended to *sryk* which fits the context well, but 1QIsaᵃ reads *zdyk* with LXX's support. V. 7, the emendations of Duhm are attractive.

7. And they shall be like a dream, a vision of the night,
   The horde of all the nations that war against Ariel,
   All that fight against her and her stronghold and distress her.

8. As when a hungry man dreams he is eating and awakes with his
      hunger unsated,
   Or when a thirsty man dreams he is drinking, and awakes
      faint with unquenched thirst.
   So shall be the multitude of all the nations that fight against
      Mount Zion.

This oracle, which is closely related to that of 17.12ff., simply
bristles with problems. Many literary critics of a past generation
tended to consider only vv. 1-4 as genuinely Isaianic because of its
note of judgment, while they regarded the remainder as a later
addition because of the elements of deliverance (Duhm, Marti).
The early form critics contested this judgment. Gressmann[57]
envisioned the writer employing older Zion tradition which
included both the elements of judgment and salvation. The
sudden transition was explained as a characteristic of the received
material with which the prophet had to work. A good number of
modern scholars have followed Gressmann's lead,[58] although one
can hardly speak of a consensus. It is obvious that one's decision
in respect to this oracle will strongly influence his understanding
of Isaiah's use of the Zion tradition.

There are several immediate problems from a literary critical
point of view which have long called forth attention. First of all,
the passage appears to have undergone some secondary expansion:
v. 4b parallels 4a, and v. 8 duplicates v. 7. Of course, this feature
might be reckoned to poetic parallelism, but such close reduplica-
tion is unexpected and especially prosaic in v. 8. Again, v. 5
causes problems by its present position within the oracle, which
anticipates the intervention of Yahweh in v. 6. Gressmann and
Procksch feel constrained to move v. 5 to a new position, either
after v. 6 or v.8. Usually the difficult reading in v. 5 of 'strangers'
(*zārāyikh*) is emended to 'foes' (*ṣārāyikh*); however, it is advisable

---

[57] Gressmann, *Der Messias*, pp. 100ff.
[58] von Rad, *Old Testament Theology*, II, p. 158; Rohland, *op. cit.*, p. 162,
pictures a more complex development. He considers vv. 1-4 to be an original
threat which has been combined by a redactor into a larger unit using a
fragment (5abα) and other verses. Nevertheless, he holds the elements of
promise for genuinely Isaianic.

to follow the LXX and 1QIsaᵃ and read 'proud ones' (*zēdhîm*).
The combination with 'tyrants' (*'ārîṣîm*) is common (Isa. 13.11;
Ps. 86.14) in describing the wicked within Israel. Then one might
see v. 5 as supplying part of the reason for the prophetic con-
demnation of Ariel. However, the form of the verb, which
indicates future time, makes this latter suggestion unlikely. Also
the content speaks against it. The judgment in v. 6, if read without the framework of v. 5, seems clearly directed against Jerusalem. The sense of the verb 'to be visited' is difficult to determine.
The phrase 'to be visited by Yahweh' occurs both in a good and a
bad sense, although in the niphal it is predominantly in the latter
sense (Num. 16.29; Isa. 24.22; Prov. 19.23). Moreover, the theophanic accompaniment points in this same direction. The tradition designates Yahweh as graciously leading his people (Pss. 68;
78; Hab. 3), but the fire, whirlwind, and storm are signs of his
anger which are directed against his enemies (Pss. 77; 97; Nahum
1; Hab. 3. 14). He does not visit graciously with these means. For
these reasons many commentators (Marti, Cheyne, Scott) include
vv. 5b-6 with vv. 1-4 as forming an oracle of judgment directed
against Jerusalem.

If one turns to the form critical problems, these are no less
difficult. The beginning of the oracle appears to follow the
typical pattern of the familiar invective-threat. The woe is
directed against Ariel and is not simply an exclamation. The
imperative in v. 1b, which urges the festal cycle to continue un-
disturbed, is used ironically against the well-regulated cult centre
and serves as grounds for the impending judgment. Since Isaiah
frequently has Yahweh pronounce the threat, there is no com-
pelling reason to suggest here that the prophet is speaking. There
is no real transition to the first person Yahweh speech of vv. 2ff.
which pronounces the threat. V. 4 does not offer any note of
repentance which might form a transition to deliverance. In spite
of the introduction of Yahweh in the third person, v. 6 could serve
as the concluding line of the judgment. However, in its present
form v. 5 introduces the decisive turnabout in events, and
Yahweh's judgment now is directed against Israel's enemies who
combat Ariel. The final verses, which are spoken to Ariel, serve
as a promise of deliverance. They are dependent on vv. 1-4 and
could not ever be considered an independent oracle.

In spite of some similarity in content, form critically speaking, the oracle in ch. 29 is completely different from that in 17.12ff. The latter is structurally a unity which moves smoothly from the threat directed to the enemy to the deliverance for Israel. In contrast to this, 29.1-4 is an invective-threat with Yahweh as the enemy of Ariel; then suddenly the oracle shifts to the form of a promise to Ariel with Yahweh now playing the role of deliverer. Few modern scholars would want to defend the earlier literary critical axiom that the pre-exilic prophets spoke only judgment, and therefore all words of promise are to be considered *a priori* as secondary. Nevertheless, such an abrupt transition from judgment to promise after the manner of 29.1-8 is most unusual in the primary level of Isaianic material. As we shall see below, the genuine Isaianic promise occurs usually within a different setting. Moreover, to argue that the abruptness in the transition stems back to the level of oral tradition is not convincing because, in the other examples of the Zion tradition, the transition is completely different in character and not disconnected (cf. Isa. 17.12ff.; Ps. 46; etc.). The unity could only be maintained by supposing that Isaiah consciously altered the Zion tradition by expanding the traditional threat into a prophetic invective. Now we have returned to the initial point of departure which was to show that the form is not at all typical of Isaiah. The evidence for supposing that the present form resulted from a conscious effort of the prophet is negative.[59]

From the perspective of traditio-criticism there are also difficulties in assuming the unity of vv. 1-8. On closer examination, the circle of tradition underlying the threat against Ariel is distinct from that of the Zion tradition which does appear in the latter verses. The threat in 1-4 is pictured as a long and protracted siege which slowly brings the populace to its knees, whereas in the Zion tradition the threat is of a sudden assault by a phantom

[59] Rohland's attempt, *op. cit.*, pp. 168ff., to overcome the inner tension of the unit by suggesting that Isaiah saw the same event from two completely different aspects—Yahweh brings the destructive flood, but he also has established Zion impregnable to attack—does not seem to be a satisfactory solution. A somewhat similar position, although more traditional, is defended by J. Schreiner, *Sion-Jerusalem*, p. 256. He argues as a major thesis that the ambivalence of Isaiah stems from the fact that he views Jerusalem both as a political capital and as the spiritual abode of Yahweh. As a political entity the city receives only judgment, but as spiritual Zion it is given promise. However, this simple polarity is not evident in this text, nor does it come to grip with the complexity of Isaiah's message elsewhere.

army or by cosmic disorder. Again the portrayal of Yahweh's judgment in v. 6 seems akin to 1-4 and distinct from the motifs of the genuine Zion tradition. The theophanic appearance of Yahweh who comes to execute judgment in flaming fire is an element from the holy war tradition which is different from his role in the Zion tradition. Here Yahweh dwells in Zion, and protects his city against the aggressive assaults of the enemy. The miraculous scattering of the enemy 'like passing chaff'—suddenly they are no more—is a somewhat different picture than the theophanic destruction, although fire does play a minor role in the Zion tradition as a protective ring around Jerusalem on occasion (Zech. 2.5; cf. Isa. 31.9). Finally, the besieged city in v. 1 with its busy cult is designated only as the place where once David encamped. It is not the holy city in which Yahweh has his eternal abode.[60]

To summarize: The combined evidence points quite clearly to the fact of two different layers in vv. 1-8. The primary oracle (vv. 1-4, 5c-6) was an invective-threat directed against Jerusalem. A secondary level (5a, b, 6) transformed the oracle into a promise by adding a word of threat to the nations which was drawn from the language of the older Zion tradition.[61]

7. Isaiah 31. 4-9

4. For thus Yahweh said to me,
   As a lion or a young lion growls over his prey,
   And though a band of shepherds be called out against him,
   He is not terrified by their cries, nor cowed by their shouts,
   So will Yahweh of Hosts come down to do battle against
   Mount Zion and its hill.

5. Like fluttering birds, so will Yahweh of Hosts protect Jerusalem.
   He will protect and deliver, spare and rescue.

6. Turn to him from whom you have completely revolted, O people of Israel.

[60] Cf. O. Procksch, *op. cit.*, p. 371, and M. Noth, 'Jerusalem und die Israelitische Tradition', *GSAT*, p. 182.
[61] Hayes' conclusions, *op. cit.*, p. 425: 'Isaiah used the common Zion tradition of the city's invulnerability to support the people' does not reckon sufficiently with the different levels of tradition within the book of Isaiah.

7. For in that day every one will cast away his idols of silver and his idols of gold which your hands have sinfully made.

8. And Assyria shall fall by a sword, not of man;
   And a sword, which is not human will devour him,
   And he will flee away before the sword, and his young men shall be enslaved.

9. His rock will slip away through terror, and his officers desert the flag in panic.
   An oracle of Yahweh who has a fire in Zion and a furnace in Jerusalem.

Most critical commentators are agreed that this passage is not of one piece, but in the method of detailed analysis there remains much disagreement. The passage is set apart from vv. 1-3 by its introductory formula as well as by its content since Jerusalem plays no role in the former oracle. The oracle also contains a familiar closing formula. However, the form and content dispel any initial impression of a unified passage. Vv. 6-7 fall out of the scheme immediately by word of warning, followed by an eschatological picture of idol rejection (cf. 2.20).

Far more serious are the problems in vv. 4-5. The initial difficulty arises from the obscurity of the figures used. Skinner (*loc. cit.*) summarized the problem many years ago precisely. If the figure of the lion crouching over its prey is taken to be a word of promise which expresses Yahweh's determination to defend Jerusalem against the Assyrians, then the interpretation results in an exact reversal of the normal usage of these figures. The lion protects his prey and the shepherds seek to destroy it! The several attempts which have been suggested to avoid this basic difficulty have not altered the anomaly. Moreover, it is quite clear from the parallels that the verb with its preposition (*lişbo' 'al*) can only mean 'to fight against' (Isa. 29.7, 8; Num. 31.7; Zech. 14.12). Yahweh is pictured attacking and not defending Jerusalem. Finally, in the great majority of cases within Isaiah the formula 'thus Yahweh said to me' introduces a threat rather than a promise.[62] In summary, the evidence points conclusively to taking v. 4 as a threat

[62] Isa. 8.5; 21.16; 31.4; Cf. 5.9; 22.14. The formula shows a complex history. The grouping around chapters 6 and 8 seems to point to a special *Denkschrift*.

against Jerusalem. Yahweh is pictured as a lion, growling over his prey, and not frightened off by the shouts of would-be rescuers.

While it remains a problem of how precisely to understand the figure of the fluttering birds (v. 5), the commentary removes all doubt that this is meant as an image of protection: 'Yahweh will guard, protect, and spare Jerusalem.' The threat against Assyria in 8a appears to be a continuation of this same thought and is a familiar note in Isaiah's message. For our purposes the difficulty in the subsequent shift of the image in 8bf. can be by-passed. The crucial issue is how to regard the juxtaposition of the threat in v. 4 with the promise in v. 5. Modern critics are much more cautious than an earlier generation in automatically assigning words of promise to the exilic period. The criteria for such judgments in assigning dates are far too subjective. Still some relative distinctions seem called for in this instance. V. 5 appears to be dependent on v. 4 which it closely parallels. It could hardly be an independent oracle which was only later attached. Moreover, v. 5 does not describe a subsequent action, or offer any bridge from threat to promise. Rather, it provides a framework for reinterpreting and transforming v. 4 into a word of promise. Such a phenomenon is a clear indication that v. 5 is of younger origin than v. 4 and serves as a corrective commentary upon it. It represents a later stage of interpretation which has modified the original words of prophetic judgment. The final verse in this secondary level—a fire in Zion and a furnace in Jerusalem—seems to make use of the Zion tradition and pictures his fire as protective for Israel, but consuming against the enemy.

8. Isaiah 14.28-32[63]

28. In the year of the death of King Ahaz came this oracle:

29. Do not rejoice, O Philistia, all of you, that the rod which beat you is broken,
    For from the serpent's root will come forth a viper, and its fruit will be a flying-serpent;

---

[63] Text criticism of Isa. 14.28-32: V. 30a appears out of order, and has been placed after 32 in the translation. Read *whymt* instead of first person. V. 31, read *môdhēdh* with 1QIsaᵃ. Cf. Begrich's more radical suggestions, *GSAT*, pp. 121ff.

30b. And he will kill your root with famine and what remains he will slay.

31. Wail, O Gate, cry out, O City, melt in fear, O Philistia, all of you,

For smoke comes out of the north, and no one can number his ranks.

32. And what should one answer the messengers of the people? 'That Yahweh has founded Zion, and in her the afflicted of his people find refuge.

30a. And the first-born of the poor feed, and the needy lie down in safety.'

This is another controversial passage; however, for our present purpose, many of the problems can be omitted. In our opinion, Begrich has correctly analysed the basic structure of the oracle and confirmed the originality of the setting given in the super-scription.[64] The oracle contains a prophetic warning against the premature rejoicing of Philistia, which had been evoked by the death of some great Assyrian king.[65] It also contains a word of instruction to Judah on how to answer in faith the emissaries of Philistia who seek an alliance. The oracle is marked by the stark contrast which is drawn between disaster for Philistia and safety for Zion.

Fullerton, in a detailed article,[66] has questioned the genuineness of vv. 30a and 32b, chiefly by the way in which the 'poor', 'needy', and 'afflicted' are introduced. He argues that Isaiah uses the words infrequently and then only to distinguish the class of the poor against the oppressing rich. Considered from a political point of view, it seems unlikely that the prophet would argue against an alliance with Philistia for the sake of the poor who alone would find refuge in Zion. What weight would this carry with those making the decision? However, if one takes the reference to include the inviolability of Zion for all of Judah, it contradicts other clear statements of the prophet in which destruction is implied (8.14f.). Fullerton concludes that the terms must be taken in a religious sense to designate the pious in accord-

---

[64] *Ibid.* His arguments appear decisive against Fullerton and Irwin.
[65] The exact Assyrian king in question remains debatable. Cf. discussion in Donner.
[66] Fullerton, 'Isaiah 14.28-32', *AJSL* 42 (1925), pp. 1ff.

ance with the usage of the psalms in the late period. He thus rejects vv. 30a and 32b as non-Isaianic.

In our opinion, the alternatives posed by Fullerton have been cast into a new light by the deeper understanding of the role of the Zion tradition in Isaiah. Fullerton's logical argument carries weight only as long as one deals with the material as a unified system of thought without considering the depth dimension which is unveiled by the study of the history of tradition. The basic question at issue is to determine the nature of the material used in vv. 30a, 32b, and to understand its use within the present oracle. It is immediately evident that the motifs are familiar ones from the Zion tradition. The reference to Yahweh's founding of Zion appears also in Isa. 28.16 (cf. Ps. 76.2; 87.5). The strong mythical flavour of the vocabulary reflects the ancient pre-Israelite source for the tradition, which has become identified with Zion. Yahweh's city has an eternal foundation which withstands the onslaughts of the roaring sea (Ps. 46). Here the poor and needy find food and safety (Ps. 132.15). Indeed, the characteristic function of the righteous king, enthroned in Zion, is to deliver and protect the poor and needy (Ps. 72.4, 12; Isa. 11.4). Basic to the Zion tradition is the true and faithful refuge at Zion (Isa. 28.16f.; Ps. 46) against which its enemies can only be shattered. It is evident that the prophet is not attempting a new political or religious formulation, but drawing material from the ancient traditions to remind Israel of her relation to Yahweh.

In Isa. 14.32 the prophet instructs Israel in the proper answer to those who seek an alliance. The theme is typical of Isaiah's message: In Yahweh alone will his people find true deliverance. The form in which the tradition is echoed is of particular interest. The answer is not a word of promise delivered to Israel, but a confession of faith proclaimed by Israel to the nations. It is a word *from* Israel, not one directed *to* Israel. Within the form of an oracle to the nations the Zion tradition is employed both as a testimony to Yahweh's absolute sovereignty over the nations, and as a reminder to Israel of her true existence.

9. Isaiah 10.27b-34

Our treatment of this passage can be brief because our conclusions are mainly negative. Usually commentators have found in these verses a pattern of Yahweh's judgment by means of an enemy from the north (27b-32), which is then followed by his deliverance of Zion (33-34). For some commentators this is an original pattern which is paralleled to the Zion tradition in 17.12ff., while for others the deliverance is a secondary addition.

In our opinion, the evidence for this pattern in 10.27ff. is too precarious to be used with any certainty. In fact, we are much inclined to follow Kaiser's lead in seeing vv. 33-34 as the introduction to the oracle in 11.1ff. His reasons have chiefly to do with the similarity of content between the two sections. The figure of the branch being cut off is continued in 11.1. Moreover, the destruction of the forests of Lebanon (34) is not applicable as a judgment on the attacking enemy but on Israel. To this can be added the form critical observation that the particle 'behold' (*hinnēh*) is frequently used in Isaiah and elsewhere as an introduction to an independent oracle, especially for the threat (3.1; 17.1; 19.1; 24.1; 30.27), and most infrequently to form a connective between threat and promise. It is also most likely that the setting of the oracle is the earlier period of the Syrian-Ephramaic war, which places it outside the period of our particular interest.

To summarize: The study of the oracles against the nations has made very clear that there is no one form which is employed, rather that a great variety of forms are used (threat, invective, warning, private oracle, etc.). Moreover, the prophet has shown great freedom in fashioning the traditional forms to his own usage, in fact, to a far greater degree than appeared in the oracles of judgment against Israel.

Characteristic of these oracles is that usually the forms exhibit a complex structure which combined the threat with the summary-appraisal (14.14f.), or the invective with the promise, or judgment with salvation. The crucial issue is how to account for this complexity. No one theory emerged to explain adequately the situation, rather the analysis pointed to different factors at work. In several instances an initial threat against Israel was secondarily transformed into a promise either by a later literary interpolation, or by the addition of a separate oracle which provided a new framework. However, at times a complex oracle with the content of judgment and salvation appeared to reflect a primary level of Isaianic tradition which could not be separated.

Finally, a wide range of different motifs from traditional material appeared in these oracles (the theophany, Yahweh as divine warrior, enemy-from-the-north, Zion). In many the Isaianic theology of Yahweh's plan provided the framework and became the dominant force in shaping the traditions. The Zion tradition played a decisive role in these oracles. However, the analysis showed two quite distinct usages of this tradition. When it appeared in the primary level of the Isaianic oracles, it was directed against Assyria and served to emphasize the supreme power of Yahweh against all other claims. In the secondary level (the so-called non-genuine) the Zion tradition appeared in oracles of promise directed to the comfort of Israel.

C. THE ORACLES OF PROMISE

It has long been observed by critical scholars that the oracles of promise play a subordinate role in the primary Isaianic tradition. In fact, for some scholars of the last century it became a *petitio principii* that Isaiah spoke only words of judgment. While few interpreters would be still inclined to support this theory, it does remain a legitimate and difficult task to try to separate the various layers of tradition which are found in the oracles of promise. Once again, the scope of this essay will be limited to those passages which are related to the Assyrians.

There is a broad agreement among most critical commentators in judging a sizeable number of passages as secondary. The following are included: 10.20-27; 29.17-21; 30.18-26; 32.15-20; 33.1-24. Unfortunately, the term 'non-genuine' has often been employed which places a negative value judgment on all but the primary oracles. We prefer to use the term 'secondary' as a literary and historical category which attempts to establish relationships in the history of the growth of tradition. This precedent has been well established in contemporary New Testament research, especially on the Synoptic problem. Since the present concern is to isolate the primary tradition of the promise oracles, these secondary passages will be omitted and treated in another chapter. Likewise, those passages which the previous analysis has judged to be secondary expansions of oracles of judgment will be handled later (18.7; 29.5, 7-8; 31.5, 9). Finally, we intend to exclude from discussion the so-called messianic passages (9.1-7; 11.1-9) for two reasons. First, no real consensus has emerged in establishing a setting. Secondly, these passages have no direct bearing on the problem of Assyria.[67] Consistent with this conscious limitation, two other eschatological passages of considerable controversy will also be omitted (2.1-4; 28.5-6).

The analysis of the invective-threat form has already revealed indirectly that a message of promise and hope was a part of the original proclamation of the prophet Isaiah. In at least two passages (28.12; 30.15) the invective established the grounds for the indictment of Israel by quoting the prophet's own words of promise which had then been rejected by the people. Particularly when these words are joined to those of the earlier period (7.3ff.), the characteristic features of his message emerge. The words are addressed to the inhabitants of Jerusalem or its representatives rather than to a special group of the pious. The prophet counsels them to be quiet and calm,[68] and to exercise a trust in Yahweh alone for deliverance by refusing to seek support from foreign alliances. Of course, as a consequence of the flat rejection of Isaiah's message, there is an alteration in the message and a change of strategy which affects both the audience (8.16-18) and the function of the words (30.8f.).[69]

Similarly, the oracles against the nations give evidence indirectly of elements of promise in the prophet's message. In several instances the implications of deliverance for Israel by the destruction of Assyria are made explicit. Isa. 14.25 predicts that 'his (Assyria's) yoke shall depart from them and his burden from their shoulder' (cf. 18.6). Again in 17.12ff. the implications of the enemy's vanishing are evident for Israel, and are made explicit in the summary-appraisal form (14b). Moreover, the warning to Philistia employs a confession in a positive way that Yahweh affords protection in Zion for the afflicted and needy (14.30b, 32). Finally, the prophetic dirge which laments the fall of the faithful city envisions a restoration of the faithful city emerging through fiery judgment (1.21ff.).

Up to this point, elements of Isaianic promise have been

[67] Cf. A. Alt's discussion of Isa. 8.23-9.6, *Kleine Schriften* II, pp. 206ff., which seeks to find a setting in the Syrian-Ephraimic war. If his thesis is correct, this would naturally have a bearing on the earlier relation to Assyria.

[68] Von Rad, *Old Testament Theology*, II, pp. 16of., interprets this as part of the holy war tradition. C. Keller represents a different point of view in 'Das quietistische Element in der Borschaft des Jesaja', *ThZ* 11 (1955), pp. 81ff.

[69] Cf. von Rad's *Old Testament Theology*, II, pp. 41ff., for a full discussion of the problem.

analysed, but without the formal structure of the promise. Can one speak of the form of promise as playing a part in primary Isaianic tradition? There is one passage at least in which this is certainly the case, namely 28.16, 17a.

16. Thus says the Lord Yahweh:
    Behold, I am laying in Zion for a foundation a stone,
    A tested stone, a precious corner stone of sure foundation.
    He who believes will not be in haste.

17. And I will make justice the line
    And righteousness the plummet.[70]

The form critical reasons for holding these verses to have been originally independent of the threat (14ff.) have already been presented. It remains an open question whether the oracle has been retained in its entirety. The introductory formula (v. 16) was also an integral part in the threat, and the formula now forms an evident seam which joins the units. The oracle seems unusually short to be complete and has an abrupt ending. It is not without precedent that an oracle of promise include a word of indictment against the enemy (Jer. 30.18ff.), so that it is possible for some ending which paralleled 17b to have served as the conclusion.

The oracle begins with the messenger formula 'thus says Yahweh', which is familiar from the threat form. As we have argued above, this formula is never preceded by an invective in an oracle of promise, but occasionally by a warning (*Mahnwort*) which is the analogous form.[71] The speech of Yahweh containing the promise is introduced by a *hinnēh* particle (behold) plus the participle and is followed by a perfect waw consecutive.[72] This

---

[70] Text critical notes on Isa. 28.16-17a: Commentators are still divided on whether to emend the perfect *yissadh* to a participle *yōsēdh* in v. 16. There are two other places in Isaiah which read a finite verb in the same construction (29.14; 38.5), but a similar textual problem is involved. In my opinion, the thorough arguments of E. König (*Lehrgebäude* III, §3440, and *Das Buch Jesaja, ad loc.*) are convincing that the participle should be read. On *bōhan* L. Koehler [*ThZ* 3 (1947), pp. 390ff.] argues for a technical Egyptian loan word which denotes a particular stone used in statues. Cf. the strictures of K. Galling, *Verbannung und Heimkehr (Festschrift Rudolph)*, (Tübingen, 1961), p. 73. V. 16b, *mûssādh* is often taken as a dittography. *yāhîš;* has often been emended unnecessarily. Cf. the significant textual evidence in the *Manual of Discipline* VII, 7, which is cited by Galling.

[71] K. Koch, *Was ist Formgeschichte* (Neukirchen-Vluyn, 1964), p. 238.

[72] Paul Humbert, 'La formule hébraïque en *hineni* suivi d'un participe', *Opuscules d'un Hébraïsant* (Neuchatel, 1958), pp. 54ff.

combination is used for words of judgment with Yahweh as
the subject in the majority of instances; nevertheless, its use
as an introduction to a promise is common (Jer. 30.18ff.; 31.7,
etc.).

Now a distinction within the promise oracle arises in terms of
the object of the oracle. The words can be directed to an addressee
in the second person, either to an individual or people, as a pledge.
Thus both Hezekiah (Isa. 38.5f.) and Zedekiah (Jer. 34.4ff.) are
encountered directly with words of promise which follow a
messenger formula. However, the oracle can also be without a
direct addressee with the emphasis falling on the action itself
(Isa. 43.19ff.), or the oracle can be directed to an addressee in the
third person (Jer. 32.26ff.). This variation is not unexpected since
a similar situation is found in the threat. In Isa. 28.16 the promise
is in the form of a proclamation without a direct addressee. The
emphasis falls on Yahweh's deed rather than serving as a word of
comfort to a segment within Israel.

The majority of oracles which are paralleled to the promise
oracle in Isa. 28.16f. are found in the book of Jeremiah. What is
surprising is the lack of any close parallels in I Isaiah, even if one
includes secondary tradition. The form of the promise which we
have analysed does not appear elsewhere outside of the prose
appendix (ch. 36f.). Isa. 10.24ff. follows closely the completely
different pattern of the salvation oracle (*Heilsorakel*). Other
secondary oracles of promise, such as 10.20ff; 29.17ff., etc. also
diverge sharply from the pattern and employ another set of
formulae. This fact would seem to indicate that although the form
was old and known to Isaiah, it played a minor role both in his
own preaching as well as in the secondary development of the
tradition.

If we turn now to the content of the oracle, it is evident that
the image to describe the work of Yahweh has been drawn from
the ancient building practice of laying a foundation stone on
which to construct the building. The imagery[73] is continued in
v. 17a when describing the construction tools of the builder as
justice and righteousness. The frequently repeated interpretation
may be correct which understands the words: 'He who believes

---

[73] The metaphorical interpretation is emphasized by J. Lindblom, 'Der
Eckstein in Jes. 28,16', *Interpretationes ad V.T. pertinentes S. Mowinckel* (Oslo,
1955), pp. 123ff.

will not be in haste,' as the inscription on the stone, but this identification is not explicitly made.

However, the vocabulary reflects more than just ancient building practice; it reveals also the influence of the Zion tradition. The language is familiar which describes Yahweh's laying a stone in Zion as a foundation which is immovable. Moreover, Isaiah employs the ancient tradition in a thoroughly positive sense which supports the belief in the central, unchanging role of Zion in Yahweh's plan of redemption. Yet there does seem to be included a polemic against a misunderstanding of this tradition. By placing the founding in the immanent future any view of Zion's inviolability apart from Yahweh's present purpose is excluded, and again Zion takes its proper place as a sign of the refuge which is in Yahweh (Ps. 46.1). In spite of a common opinion[74] there is no indication in the text that Yahweh seeks out the old cornerstone on which to build. Moreover, the emphasis of the passage is on the absolute stability of Yahweh's foundation. It is not on the invisibility of the new structure except to the eyes of faith, nor is the faith of the community to be identified with the stone.[75] The one who is faithful finds his stay on this stone; he need not flee away in fear. Typical of Isaiah is that the promise is not directed to a party within Israel, but the proclamation is about the nature of Yahweh's plan which calls for the response of faith from all of Israel. In the present context the promise has been fitted within the framework of the invective-threat. The contrast made is between those who seek their own safety through clever pacts, which is a false security, and the true safety of Yahweh in Zion. Isaiah is not thereby spiritualizing the term Zion, but he is insisting on understanding Zion as the righteous establishment of God.

To summarize: Oracles of promise play a subordinate role in the primary Isaianic tradition which relates to the Assyrian crisis. In large part, this fact stems from the overt rejection by Israel of the basis for salvation. In the one clear use of the oracle of promise, the message is consistent both with that of the invective-threat and the oracles against the nations. Yahweh has a plan of salvation—the image is of a new building in Zion—which will withstand all onslaughts for those who partake of his refuge.

---

[74] H. Gressmann, *Der Messias*, p. 109.
[75] *Contra* S. Mowinckel, *He That Cometh* (Nashville, 1955 and Oxford, 1956), p. 135, and others.

Chapter summary: The attempt has been made in this chapter to understand the message of Isaiah in the face of the Assyrian crisis by recovering the earliest levels of the tradition within his oracles. It is hoped by this means to gain an historical perspective from which one may better understand the later developments in the history of the tradition.

The message of Isaiah is cast within a limited number of stereotyped forms. Within these traditional structures certain major emphases of the prophet have emerged with clarity: a threat of judgment is directed to unfaithful Israel, a message of failure and defeat is hurled against proud Assyria, Zion as God's abode is proclaimed inviolable against the fiercest attacks of its enemies, the response of faith as quiet trust is assured the safety of Yahweh. However, these recurrent themes do not build a complete system of political or theological thought. There are no Isaianic principles which let themselves be extrapolated from the particular form of the oracle as it was delivered in a specific situation. Therefore, utmost care must be exercised in not generalizing into a broad theory a message which had a limited use. Much of the former scholarly discussion on Zion's alleged inviolability failed to pay close enough attention to the contexts in which such elements appeared.

Again there are obvious gaps and tensions in the primary tradition. Many of the questions which interest historians have not been adequately illuminated. It remains perplexing how to relate the message of unmitigated disaster to sinful Israel with the assertions of Zion's inviolability and Assyria's defeat.[76] Because these links are missing in the primary level, it is most ill advised to attempt to ease the tensions or fill in the gaps. This cannot be done either by suggesting psychological changes in the prophet, positing an earthly and spiritual Jerusalem, or postulating several different invasions. Such methodological errors blur the evidence to such an extent that no history of the tradition is possible. Only by observing the process within the developing tradition by which the tensions are overcome, the gaps filled, and logical conclusions drawn, can the real history of tradition be uncovered.

[76] The ambivalence in Isaiah's message has been described somewhat differently from that suggested by T. Vriezen, *Jahwe en zijn Stad* (Amsterdam, 1962), who emphasizes the role of the inaugural vision in holding together the elements of judgment and salvation. I agree with Vriezen in his criticism of Pedersen's explanation of the tension, cf. *Israel* III-IV, pp. 552f.

III

THE NARRATIVES OF II KINGS 18-19
(ISAIAH 36-37)

A. ACCOUNT A: II KINGS 18.13-16

13. And in the fourteenth year of King Hezekiah, Sennacherib, king of Assyria, came up against all the fortified cities of Judah and captured them. 14. Then Hezekiah, king of Judah, sent to the king of Assyria at Lachish, saying, 'I have done wrong; withdraw from me; whatever you impose upon me I will bear.' So the king of Assyria required of Hezekiah, king of Judah, three hundred talents of silver and thirty talents of gold. 15. So Hezekiah gave him all the silver that was found in the house of Yahweh, and in the treasuries of the king's house. 16. At that time Hezekiah stripped the gold from the doors of the temple of Yahweh, and from the doorposts which Hezekiah, king of Judah, had overlaid and gave it to the king of Assyria.

The account of Hezekiah's capitulation to Sennacherib appears in the Old Testament only in II Kings 18.13-16. The fact that vv. 14-16 are lacking in the parallel passage in Isaiah has evoked much debate. Since it is impossible to determine with any certainty the cause for the omission, it seems idle to construct a theory on an alleged motivation.[1] The style of the account is that

---

[1] It has usually been suggested by commentators that the Isaianic text was purposely abbreviated, the motives for which are variously explained (cf. Meinhold, *op. cit.*, p. 58). This theory remains dubious since no other clear examples of intentional abbreviation are to be found. II Kings 20 // Isa. 38 has often been cited as an example because of the shorter text in Isaiah, but the evidence for establishing the direction for the change has not been conclusive (cf. Montgomery for a characterization of the Kings excess). Olmstead was one of the first to recognize the difficulty with the theory of abbreviation [*AJSL* 31 (1915), pp. 196ff.]. He argued that, if the Hebrew text used by Isaiah had contained II Kings 18.14-16, the Isaiah redactor would certainly have copied it. Moreover, the form and content speak strongly against these verses being a post-LXX expansion. Therefore, he suggested that the Isaiah text was earlier in type and, like the Chronicler, could not have been copied from the text of Kings. However, in our opinion, the evidence does not support this hypothesis regarding the Isaiah text. It appears to be of the same text type as Kings and not the result of a later process of recensional conformity (cf. Excursus II). This leaves as the most plausible alternative by which to explain the omission of Isaiah the possibility of an inner Hebrew textual corruption. A case of haplography was caused by the recurrence of

of the Deuteronomistic historian (Dtr.) who has obviously used older sources, but who has expressed himself in his own style. Note, for example, the parallels with I Kings 14.25ff.; II Kings 18.9ff. In other words, these verses are narrative prose, typical of the author, and not just a copy from an entry in a state archive.

The attempt to establish the inner relationship of the verses has occupied considerable attention of the commentators.[2] Because v. 13 has a parallel in Isa. 36.1, the suggestion has been made that v. 13 was originally connected to v. 17, and that vv. 14-16 are an insertion which was not in the manuscript copied by Isaiah. The textual problem involved in this theory has already been discussed.[3] In respect to the literary question, vv. 14-16 could not have stood without some sort of introduction which gave the background of the capitulation. Therefore, to separate v. 13 from what follows seems improbable. It serves an integral part in the story. In this regard, an old crux arises concerning the date formula in v. 13. Since the issue has been discussed at length by most commentators,[4] it will not be necessary to recapitulate the arguments. If the formula is secondary as we tend to feel, the relation of the rest of the verse to 14-16 is not affected.

The question of the unity of vv. 14-16 has also been raised. Stade[5] recognized a break at the beginning of 16 which he thought indicated a source different from 14-15. More recently Montgomery[6] has defended the view that the phrase which begins v. 16

the identical verb at the beginning of vv. 14 and 17. While this remains only a suggestion, the difficulties inherent in the other explanations add considerable weight to its probability.

[2] Cf. Honor, *op. cit.*, pp. 36ff.

[3] Cf. the footnote above. An additional argument was first suggested by Kuenen that the shorter form of the name Hezekiah, found in vv.14-16, confirmed the theory of its intrusion between vv. 13 and 17 which share the longer form. However, Kuenen was dependent on the *ben Ḥayim* text. In the *ben Asher* text (*BH³*) v. 13 reads the shorter form. In addition, the spelling is not uniform throughout the chapter (cf. 18.1, 10).

[4] Briefly stated, the problem is how to reconcile the attack on Jerusalem by Sennacherib in 701 which in II Kings 18.13 is given as the 14th year of Hezekiah's reign with the chronology of his accession given in II Kings 18.1. No consensus has emerged on how the problem should be resolved. Either the date in II Kings 18.13 is seen as a scribal miswriting of '24' (Rowley), or it is a secondary calculation of Dtr. influenced by the statement of 15 years in 20.6 (the majority), or it is a correct date and is to be preferred over II Kings 18.1 (Albright).

[5] B. Stade and F. Schwally, *The Book of Kings* (Leipzig, 1904), p. 270.

[6] J. A. Montgomery, 'Archival Data in the Book of Kings', *JBL* 53 (1934), pp. 46-52.

'in that time' (*bāʿēth hahî'*) was a widespread archival expression of official scribes, and appears to have replaced some definite date entry. A study of all the occurrences of this expression indicates a much greater variety in function than Montgomery recognized.[7] The expression, when it stands at the head of a sentence, often indicates a break in the continuity of events caused by some new factor. However, the major function of the phrase appears to be one of synchronizing events, often quite loosely, rather than to serve as a substitution for an exact chronological item. This would indicate that v. 16 was originally a separate event which has been synchronized with the incidents which preceded. It is impossible to determine whether the compiler was using two different sources, such as state and temple archives, or merely two separate entries from one source.

Of course, the factor which has evoked the most interest in the study of this passage is the close parallel found in the Assyrian annals. According to his annals Sennacherib conducted eight military campaigns. His third campaign included an attack on Jerusalem in 701. The annal which describes this campaign has passed through a number of editions, and also appears in a number of slightly differing copies. The several editions have been studied by Honor,[8] and are given in convenient summary by Luckenbill[9] in his publication of the Oriental Institute Prism inscription. The most recent prism discovered in 1952, and now in the museum of Bagdad, is listed by C. van Leeuwen.[10] For our present purposes the minor variations in the editions are inconsequential, and the recent translation of Oppenheim[11] of the Oriental Institute Prism will be fully adequate.

[7] The phrase can modify a substantive (Num. 22.4; Judg. 4.4) or a verb. The use in a verbal clause varies greatly, the most important distinction being whether it introduces a sentence which is followed by the perfect (Josh. 5.2), or appears in the middle of a sentence, formed with waw cons. imperfects (I Kings 8.65). Several distinct uses of the formula in reference to the past occur: (*a*) to indicate an absolute time in the past (*damals*-Judg. 11.26; Num. 22.4); (*b*) to indicate a specific time in the past in relation to another (Deut. 1.9; Judg. 3.29); (*c*) to indicate a simultaneous time (*gleichzeitig*-II Kings 8.22; Esth. 8.9); (*d*) to indicate general time in the past (formerly—Isa. 20.2).

[8] L. Honor, *op. cit.*, pp. 1ff.

[9] D. D. Luckenbill, *The Annals of Sennacherib* (Chicago, 1924).

[10] C. van Leeuwen, 'Sanchérib devant Jérusalem', *Oudtest. Studiën* XIV, 1965, p. 245.

[11] *ANET*² (1955), pp. 287f.

Columns II and III of the annal describe the third campaign. Sennacherib first marched against Syria. Luli, the king of Sidon fled. His surrender was followed by the submission of a number of small states including Ashdod, Beth-Ammon, Moab, and Edom. At Ashkelon he met opposition and was forced to attack the city. He then besieged a number of coastal cities and prepared to move against Ekron, which had deposed its king Padi, a loyal subject of Assyria, and had handed him over to Hezekiah in Jerusalem. At this point the Egyptian and Ethiopian armies appeared and a battle was fought at Eltekeh. The Assyrians claimed victory. Ekron was then successfully assaulted, the rebels punished and Padi restored to office. Next Jerusalem was besieged. Forty-six walled cities and countless villages were conquered and two hundred thousand, one hundred and fifty people along with much spoil taken. Hezekiah capitulated and sent thirty talents of gold and eight hundred of silver, with other treasures to Nineveh. His territory was also reduced and divided among the Philistine city-states.

The many areas of striking agreement between the biblical account in II Kings 18.13-16 and the Assyrian annal are evident and have been recognized, of course, ever since the first publication of the latter. Both sources are agreed upon the capture of the Judaean countryside, the capitulation of Hezekiah without an assault on the city, and, in general, on the terms of the tribute.[12] Other problems are raised, however, by the failure of the annal to mention Lachish,[13] the apparent chronological schematization of the annal which mentions the restoration of Padi before Hezekiah's capitulation, and by the inordinately high number of captives reported.[14]

If there had been no other biblical accounts of the event, few historians would have contested the high degree of historical accuracy of both accounts. As it is, the question of the complete-

[12] The variation in the amount of silver talents has evoked much debate. Some have accounted for the discrepancy by suggesting varying systems of measurement; others reckon with an Assyrian exaggeration.

[13] H. M. Gevaryahu, 'The Campaign of Sennacherib against Hezekiah and the Deliverance of Jerusalem' (Hebrew), *'Oz le-David. Studies in the Bible presented to David Ben-Gurion* (Jerusalem, 1964), pp. 354ff., attempts to harmonize this difficulty by positing two treaties. However, the evidence is not sufficient to convince.

[14] Cf. A. Ungnad, 'Die Zahl der von Sanherib deportierten Judäer', *ZAW* 59 (1942/3), pp. 199ff.

ness of the annal remains a problem. However, the essential accuracy of the facts reported seems assured by the essential agreement of the two accounts. It is generally assumed that the biblical account rests upon an archival source which preserved the material chiefly because of its concern with the temple and its treasury.

B. THE SOURCE PROBLEM OF B

There is widespread agreement that the A account (II Kings 18.13-16) is followed by material from another source. The change in style from the condensed, descriptive report of the annal to the extended, dramatic representation of events and persons is striking. Moreover, the latter account in II Kings 18.17-19.37 // Isa. 36.1-37.38 (= B account) makes no reference to the events in A, and, in fact, takes no cognizance whatever of the reported capitulation.

Beside this initial separation of source A and B, the great majority of commentators have followed the impetus of Stade[15] in maintaining a further division of the latter into two strands (B¹ and B²). The reasons for this division have been repeated so frequently by commentators and introductions that a detailed treatment seems unnecessary. Briefly summarized, the argument focuses on the close parallelism in both structure and content between the two strands, the success in isolating two complete accounts, and the historical improbability of supposing a repetition of such an occurrence, particularly in its present order.[16] The last serious attempt to contest the division and to defend the unity of B by Šanda[17] remains extremely unconvincing.

However, in spite of this general agreement regarding the presence of two sources within the B account, there remains some uncertainty in the actual execution of the analysis. The points of disagreement centre in two areas: first, in determining the ending of B¹, and secondly, in the assignment of the final verses of ch. 19. The problems are closely related and can be treated together.

---

[15] B. Stade, *ZAW* 4 (1884), pp. 173ff.

[16] J. Le Moyne, 'Les deux ambassades de Sennachérib à Jérusalem', *Mélanges Bibliques A. Robert* (Paris, 1957), pp. 149ff., attempts by means of a new source criticism to recover traditions of two Assyrian embassies to Jerusalem. The analysis which follows offers the reasons why his analysis has not seemed convincing.

[17] A. Šanda, *Die Bücher der Könige*, II (Münster, 1912), pp. 289ff.

Stade's initial insight was in recognizing in 19.9 the seam by which the two accounts were connected. He suggested that 9a related closely to the prophecy in 7. There the prophet announced that Sennacherib would 'hear a rumour' (*šāmaʿ šĕmûʿāh*), and would 'return to his own land' (*šābh lĕʾarṣô*). In v. 9 he 'hears' and 'returns'. Stade assumed that the reference to his own land had been omitted by the fusion of the two sources, but that it was implicit.

Following Stade, others[18] have attempted slight modifications of his theory. The expression 'he returned' (*wayyāšobh*) in 9b was usually taken as the beginning of the B² account, and, in accordance with the well-known Hebrew idiom, translated 'again' (cf. II Kings 1.11). This seemed to establish an excellent beginning for B². Then the conclusion of B¹ was sought at the end of 19, specifically in vv. 36ff. which reported the departure of Sennacherib back to Nineveh and his ultimate death. The B² account would then end in v. 35 with the destruction of the Assyrian army by the angel of Yahweh. This division had the merits of finding two complete strands with a beginning and ending, which did not necessitate any textual loss in v. 9b. Accordingly, this division has become standard for the majority[19]: B¹ = 18.17-19.9a, 36f.; B² = 19.9b-35.

Still certain problems remain which do not seem fully explained by this analysis. Is there really a complete source present in B²? The obvious fact that there are several independent units (19.21-28; 29-31) which have only secondarily been joined might caution one against assuming a continuous source lying at the base of the second account. Montgomery's analysis of B² tends to see a series of fragmentary oracles which form a parallel to B¹ rather than a source stratification.[20] Others have wondered whether the suggested ending of B²: 'they were all dead men', is too abrupt to conclude an account.

There is one additional factor which has remained controversial in its interpretation. Right at the alleged seam between the two

[18] Kittel, Marti, Skinner, etc.

[19] A notable exception was H. Winckler, *Alttestamentliche Untersuchungen* (Leipzig, 1892), p. 46, who arbitrarily assigned v. 9a to the second source in order to harmonize the chronology of the alleged second invasion with the reign of Tirhakah. Subsequent defenders of the two invasion theory have generally abandoned this position (cf. Bright).

[20] J. A. Montgomery, *Kings*, pp. 492ff.

sources in v. 9, there is an important textual variant. Kings reads 'he returned', 'again' (*wayyāšobh*) while Isaiah has 'he heard' (*wayyišma'*). This variant has entered somewhat into the literary discussion. Haag[21] deduces from it that this uncertainty in the tradition at least confirms that fact that *wayyāšobh* functions as a verb, rather than as an adverb, 'again'. The interesting new datum is the reading of 1QIsa[a] which retains both variants, 'he heard and returned'.[22] How is this evidence to be evaluated? In Excursus II we have outlined the reasons which prevent a clear answer. Ziegler[23] repeats a common objection when he points out the repetition of the same verb (*wayyišma'*) in the Isaiah text, but this point is not decisive. Even if the fuller reading of 1QIsa[a] were to prove original, it does not become a major factor in deciding on the source problem. It would serve to strengthen the close connection between vv. 7 and 9, which was defended by Stade, and point to the fact that the prophecy of Isaiah had been fulfilled in the rumour which caused Sennacherib's return. However, this conclusion is likely even without deciding on the textual problem. Notice the same verb 'he returned' in v. 36. Moreover, the promise and fulfillment pattern suggests that the third element of the promise, namely Sennacherib's death, belongs also to the fulfillment. Therefore, we are inclined to believe that the report of his death in v. 37 does form the conclusion of the one continuous source B[1].

The final problem arises from the fact that the information in v. 36 seems to be required by both sources. B[1] needs both a destination for Sennacherib's return in 9b as well as a setting for his death in v. 37. B[2] requires not only Yahweh's successful defence of the city (predicted in v. 32), but also the return of the Assyrian king to his own land (predicted in v. 33). The solution of this difficulty was first offered by Duhm[24] with his observation that v. 33 is disturbing in its present position. First of all, it concludes with the formula 'oracle of Yahweh' which is unexpected for an oracle in Kings which continues. Moreover, the verse is a composite of 28b and 32a, and stands in tension with the complete destruction of the Assyrians which is described in v. 35.

[21] H. Haag, *RB* 58 (1951), p. 356. Cf. C. van Leeuwen, 'Sanchérib devant Jérusalem', *Oudtest. Studiën* xiv (1965), pp. 252f.
[22] Cf. Excursus II.
[23] J. Ziegler, *JBL* 78 (1959), p. 56.
[24] B. Duhm, *Das Buch Jesaia*[3], (Göttingen, 1914), p. 247.

Therefore, v. 33 is most probably to be regarded as a secondary addition which entered with the expansion of vv. 21bff., and which was used to harmonize the return in 28b and 36 with the destruction of v. 35. This means that the B² account did not originally have a reference to the return of Sennacherib, but ended with his destruction. V. 36 belongs together with 37 as the conclusion of the B¹ account.

To summarize: The presence of two continuous parallel sources has been confirmed. The first account (B¹) has been broken off at 19.9a and resumed in vv. 36f. The second account (B²) extends from 19.9b-35, and concludes with the Assyrian destruction.

C. ACCOUNT B¹ (II KINGS 18.17-19.9a, 36f. // ISA. 36.1ff.)²⁵

17. And the king of Assyria sent (the Tartan, the Rabsaris, and) the Rabshakeh with a large army from Lachish to King Hezekiah at Jerusalem. And they/he (went up and when they came to Jerusalem they came and) stood by the conduit of the upper pool, which is on the way to the Fuller's Field. 18. (And when they called for the king) there came out to them/him Eliakim, the son of Hilkiah, who was the overseer of the palace, and Shebna, the scribe, and Joah, the son of Asaph, the recorder.

19. Then the Rabshakeh said to them, 'Say to Hezekiah, "Thus says the great king, the king of Assyria: On what do you rest this confidence of yours? 20. Do you think that merely a word of the lips is counsel and strength for war! Now on whom do you trust that you have rebelled against me? 21. (Now) it is evident that you have put your trust on Egypt, that bruised reed of a staff, which if a man lean upon it, will go into his hand and pierce it. Such is Pharaoh, the king of Egypt, to all who rely upon him. 22. But if you say to me, 'We trust in Yahweh our God,' is it not he whose high places and altars Hezekiah has removed, saying to Judah and Jerusalem, 'You shall worship before this altar (in Jerusalem)?' 23. Come now, make a wager with

---

²⁵ Text criticism of II Kings 18.17ff. Cf. Excursus II for the general problems. Important excesses in Kings are bracketed in the translation. V. 17, Isa. omits the first two names and is to be preferred. Kings is a later expanded text (cf. v. 18 in Kings LXX). 17b, the Kings MT evidences dittography (cf. again LXX). V. 20, Kings *'āmartā* is preferable. V. 24, a clumsy expression, remove *phaḥath* as a gloss with Stade and Montgomery. V. 29, first person suffix appears in many mss. V. 32, it is difficult to say why the Isa. text lacks the half line. I tend to regard it as a Kings expansion, but a loss in Isa. is certainly possible. V. 34, on the problem of Hena and Ivvah, cf. the full treatment of Orlinsky, *JQR* 30 (1939/40), pp. 45ff. V. 36, Isa. reads the better text. *hā'ām* has come in as a marginal note (also Orlinsky *contra* Montgomery).

my master, the king of Assyria: I will give you two thousand horses, if you are able on your part to set riders upon them. 24. How then can you repulse a single captain among the least of my master's servants, when you rely on Egypt for horsemen? 25. Moreover, is it without Yahweh that I have come against this place/land to destroy it? On the contrary, Yahweh said to me, Go up against this land and destroy it." '

26. Then Eliakim (the son of Hilkiah), and Shebnah, and Joah said to the Rabshakeh, 'Please speak to your servants in Aramaic, for we understand it; but do not speak to us in Judaean in the hearing of the people who are on the wall.' 27. But the Rabshakeh said to them, 'Was it to your master and to you that my master sent me to speak these words? Is it not rather to the men who are sitting on the wall, who are doomed with you to eat their own dung and to drink their own urine?'

28. Then the Rabshakeh stood up and cried with a loud voice in Judaean, and speaking said, 'Hear the word of the great king, the king of Assyria. 29. Thus says the king, "Do not let Hezekiah deceive you, for he will not be able to deliver you (out of his hand). 30. Do not let Hezekiah make you rely on Yahweh, saying, Yahweh will surely deliver us, and this city will not be given into the hand of the king of Assyria." 31. Do not listen to Hezekiah, for thus says the king of Assyria: "Make peace with me and come out to me; and eat each of you from his own vine and his own fig tree and drink the waters of his own cistern; 32. until I come and take you away to a land like your own land, a land of grain and wine, a land of bread and vineyards, (a land of olive trees and honey, that you may live and not die. And do not listen to Hezekiah when) he misleads you by saying Yahweh will deliver us. 33. Has any of the gods of the nations ever delivered his land out of the hand of the king of Assyria? 34. Where are the gods of Hamath and Arpad? Where are the gods of Sepharvaim (Hena, and Ivvah)? Have they delivered Samaria out of my hand? 35. Who among all the gods of the/these countries have delivered their countries out of my hand, that Yahweh should deliver Jerusalem out of my hand?" '

36. But the people/they were silent and did not answer him a word for the king's command was, 'Do not answer him.' 37. Then Eliakim, the son of Hilkiah, who was the overseer of the palace, and Shebna the scribe, and Joah, the son of Asaph, the recorder came to Hezekiah with their garments rent, and told him the words of the Rabshakeh.

19.1 When King Hezekiah heard it, he rent his garments and covered himself with sackcloth and went into the house of Yahweh. 2. And he sent Eliakim who was overseer of the palace and Shebna the scribe and the senior priests, covered with sackcloth to Isaiah, the prophet, the son of Amoz. 3. They said to him, 'Thus says Hezekiah, This day is a day of distress, of rebuke and of disgrace; children have come to birth, and there is no strength to bring them forth. 4. It may be that Yahweh your God has heard all the words of the Rabshakeh, whom his master, the king of Assyria, has sent to mock the living God, and will rebuke the words which Yahweh your God has heard; therefore lift up a prayer for the remnant that is left.'

5. When the servants of King Hezekiah came to Isaiah, Isaiah said to them, 'Thus you shall say to your master: Thus says Yahweh: "Do not fear because of the words that you have heard with which the servants of the king of Assyria have blasphemed me. 7. Behold, I will put a spirit in him, so that he shall hear a rumour and return to his own land; and I will cause him to fall by the sword in his own land." '

8. And the Rabshakeh returned, and found the king of Assyria fighting against Libnah, for he had heard that he had left Lachish. 9a. And when the king heard concerning Tirhakah of Ethiopia: 'Behold he has set out to fight against you', 36. then Sennacherib, king of Assyria, departing went and returned to Assyria and dwelt at Nineveh. 37. And as he was worshipping in the house of Nisroch his god, Adrammelech and Sharezer, his sons, slew him with the sword, and escaped into the land of Ararat. And Esarhaddon his son reigned in his stead.

The first task is to analyse the structure of the B¹ account as a whole. The passage consists of continuous narrative which joins together a series of speeches. It is clear that the speeches comprise the bulk of the unit and account for 23 of the 32½ verses. The narrative material which connects the speeches serves to introduce (vv. 17, 18) and conclude (19.8, 9a, 36, 37) the story. It is also used to make the main transition from the speeches of the Rabshakeh to the subsequent speeches of Hezekiah and Isaiah (18.36-19.2). The style of the connective narrative is the flat descriptive language of the historian—only once is direct discourse used (18.36)—and contrasts markedly with the colourful language of the speeches.

Turning to the speeches, the style is to be distinguished, on the one hand, from the common biblical manner of relating a story by means of direct discourse (e.g. Gen. 27; Josh. 2). The units have the formal elements of delivered speeches rather than extended conversation. On the other hand, the speeches are not homogeneous literary constructions of the author. They represent neither the long, programmatic speeches typical of Dtr. (Josh. 23; I Sam. 12; I Kings 8), nor the stereotyped response which is characteristic of the prophetic legend.[26] Rather, the speeches in B¹ reflect a variety of forms of oral tradition many of which are non-prophetic in origin, and which reveal many more signs of independent life than a literary composition. This observation suggests that a more detailed analysis of the separate units may clarify the

[26] K. Koch, *Was ist Formgeschichte* (Neukirchen-Vluyn, 1964), pp. 207ff.

exact nature of the traditions which have been preserved. Also such an analysis is necessary in pointing out the characteristics of B¹ in contrast to B².

Even a cursory examination of the Rabshakeh's first speech (18.19-25) reveals a number of perplexing problems. The speech opens with the traditional formulae which are associated with the transmission of a message. There is the call to attention which designates the addressee, 'Say to Hezekiah', followed by the messenger formula, 'Thus says the great king, the king of Assyria'. But the ensuing message seems to evidence neither the form nor the content of the traditional message. Rather, the speech oscillates between threats, taunts, and argumentation. Secondly, the change of persons within the speech makes it difficult to follow. The speech begins with the normal pattern of the message. The addressor is referred to in the first person (vv. 20, 22) and the addressee in the second (19-21). But in the middle of the unit Hezekiah is suddenly referred to in the third person; the second person address in v. 22 becomes a plural pronoun in the Kings text; the Assyrian king becomes a third person referent (24); and the first person is used for the Rabshakeh (24, 25).[27] Finally, the lack of logical consistency in the order of the argumentation has often been observed.[28] The two references to Yahweh's help (vv. 22, 25) are separated and v. 24b seems to hang very loosely with both that which precedes and that which follows.

The difficulties of the speech are not confined to formal matters, but are equally entwined into the complexity of the context. However, it seems wise to turn first to the formal problems which have been outlined. First, how is one to explain the divergence of the speech in terms of its form from the common pattern of the message? Normally, one would expect an actual message to follow the introductory formulae. For example: 'He sent messengers . . . to Ahab . . . and said to him, "Thus says Benhadad: 'Your silver and your gold are mine; your fairest wives and children also are mine.' " ' (I Kings 20. 2f.) Or, 'To the king, my lord, your servant Enurta-ilaia. The *tartan* has sent a message

[27] Cf. H. M. Gevaryahu, 'The Speech of Rab-Shakeh to the People on the Wall of Jerusalem' (Hebrew), *Studies in the Bible presented to M. H. Segal* (Jerusalem, 1964), pp. 96f., who tries to distinguish sharply between the words of the king and those of the Rabshakeh.

[28] W. Rudolph, 'Zum Text der Königsbücher', *ZAW* 63 (1951), p. 214.

thus: "Set on its way the spoil which is at your disposal." [29] In contrast to this form, the lack of an ultimatum is striking in the Rabshakeh's message. Rather than such a formal pronouncement, the speech moves into almost *ad hoc* threat and diatribe. Of course, it should be pointed out that the first speech was broken off by the protest of the Jerusalem emissaries, and that the actual appeal to surrender does appear in the second speech to the populace (v. 31). However, this correct observation does not fully alleviate the difficulty. The speech does not follow the expected pattern even from the outset. Where else can one show such freedom taken by the messenger in the transmission of his message? It is possible, of course, that this alleged freedom really lay with the Dtr. redactor. The speeches are only literary imitations of the actual situation involving a messenger. The similarity would extend only to the stereotyped introductory formulae. But as we shall argue, the nature of the content with its accurate historical setting would caution one against moving too quickly in this direction.

It is our contention that the perplexity has arisen out of a failure to execute properly the form critical analysis of this speech. The fact of the messenger formula has led quite naturally in seeking a parallel in the traditional form of the message. Is there another alternative? In his brief treatment, Westermann[30] suggests that the speech should not be regarded as simply literally transmitting a message; rather, it is 'an expanded message' (*eine entfaltete Botschaft*). This freedom to develop the essential commission stems from his role as army commander instead of being merely a messenger. Westermann's theory remains an interesting hypothesis, but without any evidence to support this role of the army commander.

In fact, the closest Near Eastern parallel suggests a somewhat different solution. The first of the Nimrud letters,[31] written to the Assyrian king by two officials, reflects a situation which is striking in its similarity to the biblical account. According to Saggs' interpretation, Ukin-zer, head of the Chaldaean tribe of Bit-Amukkani, revolted against the Assyrians. The letter deals with

[29] H. W. F. Saggs, 'The Nimrud Letters', 1952-Part II, *Iraq* 17 (1955), p. 133.
[30] C. Westermann, *Grundformen prophetischer Rede* (München, 1960), p. 77.
[31] H. W. F. Saggs, *op. cit.*, 1952-Part I, pp. 23ff.

an Assyrian effort to enlist native support against Ukin-zer.
Letter I recounts an attempt to negotiate with the city of Babylon
which was controlled by followers of Ukin-zer.

'To the king my lord your servant(s) Šamaš-bunaia (and) Nabu-
etir. . . . On the twenty-eighth we came to Babylon. We took our
stand before the Marduk-gate (and) argued with the Man of
Babylon. *So-and-so* the servant of Ukin-zer was present at his side.
When they came out they were standing before the gate with the
Babylonians. We spoke to the Babylonians in this way: "*Why* do
you *act hostilely* to us for the sake of them?", (adding): "Their
place is in the midst of *Chaldaean tribesmen* . . . Babylon indeed
shows favour to *a Chaldaean*! Your citizen-privileges have been
set down (in charter)." *I kept going* to Babylon: we used many
arguments with them. . . . They would not *agree* to come out,
they would not argue with us: they (just) kept sending us
messages. . .'

What is illuminating in the letter is the report to the Assyrian
king by his officials, who were carrying out a diplomatic assignment with a far greater role than simply transmitting his message.
Standing outside the closed city gate, the Assyrian emissaries
attempt to persuade the Babylonians by means of argument to
sever their connection with the rebels. The incident described is
that of a diplomatic disputation in which arguments are raised and
counter-arguments parried in an effort to break down the resistance. One is struck by the remarkable freedom of the officials in
using a great variety of techniques to achieve their goal. They
reason with the Babylonians. They remind them of their treaty
obligations. They seek to divide the loyalty of the city. They
become sarcastic, and attempt to ridicule or even to employ open
threats. In Letter II they even offer a special tax exemption for
anyone deserting Ukin-zer (Line Rev. 3ff.).[32]

Of course, the parallel with the Kings account is not absolute.
The Nimrud Letter I does not retain the messenger formulae, nor
show as clearly the form in which the argument was conducted.
Still the parallel is close enough to suggest common patterns
associated with the diplomatic disputation. Moreover, this hypothesis appears to bring illumination precisely to those points
which have caused difficulty in the past. First, the disputation
setting explains why the Kings passage diverges from the tradi-

[32] *Ibid.*, pp. 26ff.

tional messenger pattern. The Rabshakeh's function was not merely to transmit the message, but quite obviously to persuade and conjole. His role is not a function of his office as commander of an army, but as diplomat of the king. For this reason he has the freedom in relation to the royal message. At times he elaborates on it in his own name, but again he can abandon it completely to engage in a different line of verbal attack. The lack of one consistent line of argument would be natural in a disputation,[33] as would also the fluctuation in style between questions, imperatives, and conditionals (cf. the disputation style in Jer. 27.16ff.). Again, the Rabshakeh's position as royal diplomat would explain his proficiency with the language,[34] as well as his intimate knowledge of the internal affairs of the Judaean state.[35]

When we turn to examine more closely the content of the Rabshakeh's speech, we observe other features which accord favourably with a genuine historical setting. In v. 22 the Rabshakeh attempts to annihilate an argument of the Judaeans even before it is broached: 'But if you say to me, "We trust in Yahweh our God", is it not he whose high places and altars Hezekiah has removed?' The perplexing feature of this argument is the strange mixture between an intimate knowledge of the cultic reforms of Hezekiah and its blatant pagan point of view.[36] Only someone completely removed from the Hebrew religion could have interpreted Hezekiah's reform as an insult to Israel's deity. Even the completely syncretistic Jewish women of the exile do not share this perspective, but simply defend the need of pagan libations (Jer. 44.15ff.). It is much more difficult to assume a sophisticated literary imitation of a pagan's attitude by the Hebrew author, than the presence of genuine historical tradition.

Moreover, the automatic connection made between seeking the deity's help and the cultic sacrifice to him is a feature which reflects a genuine Near Eastern practice and not a later tendentious theological contrivance. So, for example, Tukulti-Ninurta sends

[33] A literary dislocation such as suggested by Rudolph, *op. cit.*, is still possible.

[34] E. Ullendorff, 'The Knowledge of Languages in the Old Testament', *BJRL* 44 (1962), pp. 455ff.

[35] Cf. Gevaryahu, *op. cit.*, p. 96, who goes much too far in picturing the Rabshakeh as an 'expert' in foreign affairs.

[36] Contrast this perspective with the contrived pagan posture of Achior, the Ammonite, who offers council to Holofernes, the commander of the Assyrian army in Judith 5.20f.

a message to Kashtiliash and taunts him before the battle: 'When thy pleasure in sacrificing is filled, (begin) thy battle ... unto what fastness canst thou trust, that thou mayst protect thy people? It will avail nought for thee. ...'[37] Again this element is easier to understand as genuinely historical rather than as a literary device, particularly since this is a unique element within the Dtr. history.

Finally, it is generally agreed upon that Hezekiah's reform had strong political overtones as well as religious.[38] The removal of Assyrian altars was an overt sign of rebellion. The fact that such activity came to the attention of the Assyrians would appear quite natural and would hardly need the elaborate speculation of Gevaryahu[39] who regards Jewish mercenaries as the mediators of this information.

Up to this point, we have argued for the genuine historical elements of the Rabshakeh's speech which are reflected in both its form and content. In many of the older literary critical commentaries these ancient features have been overlooked. However, there are still elements of the oracle which have not been satisfactorily explained. The speech evidences features which seem to point to a much later date and which reveal a pattern which appears to reflect little historical verisimilitude.[40] This juxtaposition of older and younger elements in the one oracle is a characteristic of the speech which has evoked much divergent opinion among critical scholars. First of all, the Rabshakeh's reference to the reform of Hezekiah points up this strange ambivalence between older and younger elements. As we have indicated, the Assyrian diplomat argues from a genuine pagan perspective which has misunderstood completely the character of Hezekiah's religious policy. At the same time, the profile which emerges of Hezekiah is that of the Dtr. historian, who interprets the removal of Assyrian cult objects and the destruction of the foreign elements as part of a programme of cultic centralization in Jerusalem. The observation of the older literary critics that the

---

[37] R. Campbell Thompson and M. E. L. Mallowan, 'The British Museum Excavations at Nineveh, 1931-32', *Annals of Archaeology and Anthropology* 20 (1933), p. 122.

[38] E. W. Todd, 'The Reforms of Hezekiah and Josiah', *SJT* 9 (1956), pp. 288ff.

[39] Gevaryahu, *op. cit.*, pp. 98f.

[40] Cf. N. K. Gottwald, *All the Kingdoms of the Earth* (New York, 1964), pp. 190ff.

vocabulary and historical pattern associated with Josiah's reform
have strongly influenced the portrayal of Hezekiah's activities[41]
cannot be dismissed simply by reference to other genuine historical
elements in the account.

Again, a striking feature of the Rabshakeh's speech are the
quite audible echoes of the oracles of the prophet Isaiah. One
could naturally argue that the reference to the worthlessness of
the Egyptians as allies (Isa. 30.2f.) and the futility of Judah in
trusting on horses (Isa. 31.3) was so obvious as to preclude a
dependency on Isaiah. Still it is interesting that both these references are missing in the B² account. Moreover, the bold assertion
of the Assyrian: 'Yahweh said to me, go up against this land and
destroy it,' allows for no such general interpretation. The theology
is so peculiar to Isaiah (10.5ff.), and so foreign to any Near
Eastern pattern that the issue of dependency upon Isaianic
tradition cannot be avoided.[42]

Within recent years another interpretation of the Rabshakeh's
remark has been suggested which has gained increasing popu-
larity. M. Tsevat formulated it as follows: 'These words from
Rabshakeh's address ... can only mean in the mouth of the
Assyrian official that Yahweh is avenging the infraction of the
oath sworn in his name.'[43] Accordingly, this verse would not be
a later reflection of Isaiah's message, but a genuinely historical
reference to the breaking of the treaty between the Assyrians and
Ahaz which Hezekiah had effected. In our opinion, this interpretation of the text is not possible. It illustrates an increasing
tendency toward the uncritical use of the treaty pattern in situations in which the pattern is totally foreign. First of all, it is a
debatable question whether, in fact, the Assyrians did require its
vassal to swear by the vassal's own deities as well as by the
Assyrian.[44] Since the specialists in the field remain divided in

[41] Duhm, *op. cit.*, pp. 234f.

[42] Gevaryahu, *op. cit.*, p. 96, finds the closest parallel in *Die Inschriften
Asarhaddons*, ed. Borger, pp. 13, 14, which is still quite distant. The well-
known command of Kemosh to Mesha': 'Go take Nebo against Israel',
(Moabite Stone, line 14) is, of course, a different pattern.

[43] M. Tsevat, 'The Neo-Assyrian and Neo-Babylonian Vassal Oaths and
the Prophet Ezekiel', *JBL* 78 (1959), pp. 199ff.

[44] V. Korošec, *Hethitische Staatsverträge* (Leipzig, 1931), p. 95 and G. E.
Mendenhall, 'Law and Covenant in Israel and the Ancient Near East', *BA* 17
(1954), p. 60, deny it (cited by Gevaryahu, p. 97). M. Tsevat and D. J.
McCarthy, *Treaty and Covenant. A Study in Form in the Ancient Oriental Documents*

opinion, it does not seem wise to press the point. More important is the fact that nowhere in the Kings account of B[1] does the issue revolve about a broken treaty in the sense suggested by Tsevat. According to the Rabshakeh, Hezekiah's sin lies in removing the altars of Yahweh, not in profaning his name by a broken oath.[45] The explicit reference to the treaty stipulations in the Nimrud letters[46] points up the totally different context of the biblical account.

Again, the formal elements of the verse vitiate the identification with the treaty stipulations.[47] V. 25 is not a curse directed against the faithless vassal, but a private oracle to the Assyrians. This in itself presents a major difficulty with the theory. The essence of the curse in the treaty is that it works automatically, over and above any action of the offended party, to bring disaster. Nowhere is the offended party the designated agent of the curse. We reject as misleading the alleged reference to the treaty pattern as an explanation of 18.25.

Finally as another sign of the younger elements, the speech reflects a theological schematization which is also distinct from the message of Isaiah. Even a casual reader must be aware of the frequency of the word 'trust' which forms the central motif word of the unit. Within the space of seven verses the root *bṭḥ* appears seven times. In contrast to this concentration, the word appears only once in the second speech of the Rabshakeh to the people, and is replaced by nine occurrences of the new catchword 'save' (*nṣl*). Although the verb 'to trust' does occur in Isaiah's theology (cf. 30.15) it is a more central term in the theology of the Dtr. historian and serves specifically as the rhubric under which Hezekiah is characterized (II Kings 18.5).

To summarize: The first speech of the Rabshakeh has its setting in the diplomatic disputation and reflects a level of ancient historical tradition. However, there is another level of the oracle which is much younger and indicates later theological reflection on the tradition.

---

and in the Old Testament (Rome, 1963), p. 79, affirm it. Cf. D. J. Wiseman, 'The Vassal Treaties of Asarhaddon', *Iraq* 20 (1958), pp. 22f.

[45] This point has already been made by Gevaryahu, *op. cit.*, p. 97, note 16.

[46] Saggs, *op. cit.*, Letter I, pp. 23f.

[47] For a recent study of the subject, cf. D. R. Hillers. *Treaty-Curses and the Old Testament Prophets* (Rome, 1964).

The first speech of the Rabshakeh is interrupted by the protest of the Judaean emissaries. They urge him to speak in the diplomatic language of Aramaic instead of Hebrew, which was being overheard and understood by the people on the wall. The biblical account reflects with remarkable accuracy elements of a scene which could hardly have arisen apart from genuine historical tradition. The crude answer of the Assyrian fits exactly into the setting of the disputation which has been sketched above. By their consternation, the emissaries only play into the hands of the experienced Assyrian negotiator. His role is not merely to communicate a message, but rather to persuade and agitate. He reacts immediately to the new situation, and far from complying to the request, appeals directly to the populace in an attempt to arouse support against Hezekiah's position.

The form of the speech evidences many of the same problems which were encountered in the first. Twice the Rabshakeh introduces the message of the king with the messenger formula (vv. 29, 31). Following the first is a series of warnings with a parallel structure, each admonishing the people against any reliance on Hezekiah's words. The freedom of the speaker to interject admonitions befitting the new situation confirms the Rabshakeh's role as a disputant. The use of the third person 'from his hand' (*miyyādhô*) may be simply a textual corruption, but it could reflect the same fluctuation of persons which appeared above. The actual message of the king comes in v. 31. It is the offer of the terms of capitulation which have been made as attractive as possible under the circumstances and gives evidence of the same clever diplomatic skill found in Tiglath-Pileser's approach to the Babylonian rebels some thirty years before.[48] Hallo,[49] in reference to the parallel, points out some of the positive aspects of the Assyrian policy of resettlement which have been overlooked by the earlier commentators who found it odd for the exile to have been mentioned at all. Nevertheless, the threat of death for those refusing (v. 32) places the offer in its proper setting: live and not die!

The difficulties of the second speech increase measurably after 32b. First, there are several perplexing textual problems. The Isaiah parallel to v. 32 has a text which lacks half a line. Moreover,

---

[48] Saggs, *op. cit.*, *Iraq* 17 (1955), p. 47; 18 (1956), p. 56.
[49] W. W. Hallo, 'From Qarqar to Carchemish', *BA* 23 (1960), p. 59.

in v. 34 the final half line, 'Have they delivered Samaria out of my hand?', does not connect smoothly with the first half. Scholars[50] are divided on whether to accept the additional phrase of the Lucian text: 'Where are the gods of the land of Samaria?' In addition to this, there is a literary problem which has long been noticed. The extended reference in 32bff. to Hezekiah's misleading the people in trusting Yahweh seems out of place. It would have been far more natural for it to have come after v. 30, and for the speech to have concluded with the threat in 32a. The change in tone from 32bff., with its direct attack on Yahweh's power to save, accords poorly with v. 25, in which the Rabshakeh claims the support of Yahweh for his enterprise. Again, the verses in question seem closely dependent on those of the B[2] account, 19.11ff. Particularly for these latter reasons Duhm[51] and a number of literary critics have concluded that vv. 32bff. are a secondary addition to the original oracle in which the note of blasphemy from the second account has been interjected into the first.

In spite of the initial logic of this move, there are some real difficulties involved in the theory. Vv. 32bff. do not show a literary dependency on 19.11ff. There is an obvious core of common tradition, but the variations are such that direct dependency is highly improbable. Again, if vv. 32bff. are excised as secondary to the oracle, it is difficult to explain the reaction of Hezekiah in 19.4: 'the words of the Rabshakeh . . . to mock the living God'. Finally, the lack of a strictly logical order appeared as a characteristic element also of the first speech. We are, therefore, inclined to suggest that these problems cannot be solved simply on the literary level.

In the analysis of the first speech, the point was made that the oracle presented two distinct faces, an older and a younger. These different elements could be described, but not separated by literary operation. A similar situation now appears for the second speech. Up to now the analysis has concentrated on those elements of genuinely ancient, historical tradition. But the quality of the

[50] Klostermann was the first to argue for its originality. He has been followed by most of the recent commentators (Kittel, Burney, Šanda, *BH*). On the other hand, Rahlfs, *Septuaginta-Studien*, III (Göttingen, 1911), p. 278, argued that the verse is a secondary accretion. His opinion is accepted by Montgomery, *Kings*, p. 503. Orlinsky, *op. cit.*, pp. 46f., has argued strongly for its originality against Rahlfs. We are inclined to accept Orlinsky's conclusion.   [51] Duhm, *ad loc.*

tradition changes from v. 32b onward to reflect the later theological concerns of the Dtr. historian.

The issue turns about the use of the tradition of the blasphemy
of God (*Gotteslästerung*). There can be little doubt that Israel's
reflection on the problem of the blasphemy against Yahweh underwent considerable change in the course of its history. Due to the
lack of any full scale treatment on the subject, it is necessary to
trace some of the main lines of the development. One of the
earliest occurrences of the term to 'defy' God (*ḥrp*, chiefly piel)
comes in the account of David and Goliath (I Sam. 17.45). This
story which became the illustration *par excellence* of the blasphemy
of God may well indicate the original setting for the tradition.
The scene is the confrontation of two armies. A champion
emerges and, according to the ancient custom of the contest, lays
down the challenge. In his speech to the enemy Goliath defies
the army (17.10) and baits them with taunts. Yet already within the
same chapter the object of the blasphemy has shifted from
'defying the armies of the living God' (v. 26) to defying God himself (v. 45).

This same pattern in which the interpretation of the words of
blasphemy involves a shift of emphasis can be seen in the prophetic oracles. The usual form is that of the invective threat. The
words of the enemy are repeated to form the grounds for his
judgment by means of a subordinate clause. This is then followed
by the divine threat, often introduced by a messenger formula and
given in the first person. 'Because (*ya'an*) you said: "These two
nations . . . shall be mine, and we will take possession of them,"
therefore, says Yahweh God, I will deal with you according to the
anger and envy which you showed . . . you magnified yourself
against me with your mouth, and multiplied words against me'
(Ezek. 35.10ff., cf. also I Kings 20.28; Isa. 10.5ff.; Isa. 14.12;
Jer. 48.28ff.; Ezek. 27.3ff., 28.2ff.; Obad. 1.3ff.; etc.). The interesting factor is that in the great majority of cases the words of the
enemy are simply words of self-aggrandisement and arrogance.
Egypt says, 'I will rise, I will cover the earth' (Jer. 46.8); Tyre says,
'I am a god, I sit in the seat of the gods' (Ezek. 28.2); Edom says,
'Who will bring me down to the earth' (Obad. 1.3). Yet these
words are interpreted as direct blasphemy against Yahweh. 'You
have magnified yourself against me with your mouth' (Ezek.
35.13).

In the post-exilic period this tension between the arrogant words of the enemy and their interpretation as blasphemy against God is removed. The enemy now engages in a frontal attack on Yahweh himself. This approach is particularly clear in the book of Daniel in which the rulers of the world utter blasphemy against the Lord of heaven before they are destroyed. Nebuchadnezzar says, 'Who is the god that will deliver you out of my hands' (3.15). Belshazzar is pronounced doomed because 'you have lifted yourself against the Lord of heaven' (5.23). And in the end time the evil one is known by his 'speaking blasphemous things against the God of Gods' (11.36; cf. 7.25; 8.25).

Now it is our contention that the portrayal of Assyria as the blasphemer of Yahweh reflects these same stages of the tradition of the enemy as the blasphemer. In the oracle of Isa. 10.5ff. Assyria boasts of her power. 'Are not my commanders all kings? Is not Calno like Carchemish?' To which the prophet answers by means of a wisdom saying, 'Shall the axe vaunt itself over him who hews with it?' Assyria's sin does not occur through direct defying of Yahweh; rather, it lies in the arrogant boasting which the prophet interprets as a vaunting against God. Likewise, in the poetic oracle in II Kings 19.23. Assyria boasts: 'With my many chariots I have gone up to the heights of the mountains . . . I felled its tallest cedars', etc. But the prophet understands this boast as a mocking of Yahweh: 'Whom have you mocked and reviled? Against whom have you raised your voice and haughtily lifted your eyes? Against the Holy One of Israel!' (v. 22).

A later stage in the development of the tradition is discernible in the second account in II Kings (B²). The letter which is addressed to Hezekiah attempts to persuade him not to be deceived by Yahweh. Yahweh is characterized as the deceiver, and aligned with the gods of the nations who are powerless to save. There is no longer a distinction between the enemy's words and the prophet's interpretation, but Yahweh himself is directly attacked. Hezekiah's prayer focuses on this blasphemy of the deity: 'he has sent to mock the living God'. In the Chronicler's account the blasphemous tone of the Assyrian is increased in tone. 'He wrote letters to cast contempt on Yahweh the God of Israel and to speak against him saying, "Like the gods of the nations . . . so the God of Hezekiah will not deliver his people from my hand" ' (II Chron. 32.17). The Chronicler at this point is not far removed from the perspective of Daniel when he sees the whole Assyrian invasion as a theological problem involving the honour of Yahweh against the calumny of the enemy.

Now with this background we return to the second speech of the Rabshakeh in II Kings 18 and attempt to evaluate his use of the blasphemy tradition. It seems evident that the position expressed in 32bff. is not far removed from that of the second account in B² (19.10ff.). The Rabshakeh attacks Yahweh directly as impotent to deliver, and like B² aligns him with the gods of the nations. The tension between the words of the enemy and the subsequent interpretation as blasphemy has disappeared. The unit is all of one piece. The only friction which remains is with the positive opinion of Yahweh's role which was expressed in the first speech.[52] We do not agree with Duhm when he removes the verses as a later interpolation. This is unlikely because the framework shares the same developed tradition of blasphemy.[53] Rather, we would argue from this history of development that the Dtr. redactor has thoroughly reworked the ancient traditions with his own theological intent. The traditions which are preserved are not all of the same age. This explains why even in the B¹ account older and younger elements are juxtaposed.

The reaction to the Rabshakeh's speech to the people is registered by the prose narrative, first by the emissaries and, secondly by Hezekiah, which forms a bridge to the two final speeches. Hezekiah's great deference to the prophet is shown by his choice of messengers. His request for intercession is given with the utmost reserve and even timidity. The actual request is preceded by a type of proverbial statement (cf. Hos. 13.13; Isa. 66.7), which illustrates the desperate nature of the crisis. The prophet is left to draw the implications of the proverb: now only God can help! The author is using a stylistic device with considerable effectiveness in order to create a posture of fear and embarrassment. One is not justified with Kissane[54] to read in a sense of Hezekiah's deep sense of repentance before his due chastisement which now results from his failure to obey the earlier commands of the prophet. The actual request for prophetic inter-

---

[52] Cf. Gevaryahu's method, pp. 96f., for harmonizing the friction.

[53] Duhm is forced to strike the phrase 'to mock the living God' in 19.4. The same theme continues, however, in Isaiah's reply in 19.6.

[54] E. J. Kissane, *The Book of Isaiah*, I (Dublin, 1941), *ad loc*.

cession comes in v. 4, expressed with particular awareness of the uniqueness of his role. Hezekiah is himself in the temple, but this is immaterial before the power of the prophet's intercessary prayer to his God. The grounds for hope in Yahweh's intervention lie not in the covenantal relation, but in the injured honour of God through the blasphemous words of the Rabshakeh. The prophet's response is given in simple straightforward prose. The message from Yahweh is for him not to fear. God will effect both Sennacherib's retreat and his death.

One of the usual manners of interpreting this passage is to contrast this picture of the 'Isaiah of legend' with the 'real Isaiah', the eighth-century prophet. S. Blank[55] represents an extreme form of this attitude when he characterizes the portrait of Isaiah in II Kings 19 as 'shaped almost wholly by the popular mind ... a barely recognizable shadow of the historical Isaiah'. There are several difficulties with this position, in our opinion. Usually this sharp dichotomy is achieved only by first assuming the role of the historical Isaiah to be completely transparent. He was a lone social reformer, divorced from the cult who demanded justice for the oppressed, and complete destruction to the sinful nation. This is an obvious caricature of the 'liberal Isaiah' which has eroded a good bit in recent years. Nevertheless, the point which is being emphasized is that the role of the historical Isaiah is not at all clear in many areas. His function as court prophet, his relation to the cultic traditions of Zion, his use of wisdom materials, remain problematic. Therefore, caution is in order against an assumption that the historical Isaiah is clearly known.

Then again, the delineation of the portrait of Isaiah in II Kings 19 as the 'Isaiah of legend' is not free from criticism. If one is using the term 'legend' in its technical form critical sense—and the term loses its precision unless we do—then it is by no means clear that the B[1] account falls into this category. Jolles[56] and Koch[57] have analysed the form as one in which the historical and even biographical elements recede in order to focus on those edifying virtues or class ideals which have evoked the story. The portrayal of Isaiah does not illustrate this pattern, and stands in

[55] S. H. Blank, *Prophetic Faith in Isaiah* (New York and London, 1958), pp. 9ff.

[56] A. Jolles, *Einfache Formen*[2] (Darmstadt, 1958), pp. 23ff.

[57] K. Koch, *Was ist Formgeschichte* (Neukirchen-Vluyn, 1964), pp. 210f.

contrast with the later portrayal of Hezekiah in B² in which the
pious king is typified. In the light of these criticisms, it is necessary
to examine anew the prophetic portrayal in the Kings chapter.

Although we have criticized Blank's attempt to contrast the
portrayals of Isaiah, we are fully agreed with him that there are a
variety of pictures present. The striking fact in II Kings 19 is that
the picture of the prophet's role does not give the impression of a
recent *ad hoc* creation. Rather, the writer appears dependent on a
circle of tradition in describing an office with a stated role in which
the prophet acts as intercessor for the people before Yahweh.
He serves to mediate the needs of the people to his God, and,
in turn, to relay the message of God to the people. He offers
the comfort of God through the divine word (19.6). It is a
power-laden word which not only communicates the nature
of future events, but effects the fulfilment of the events as well
(19.36f.).

Moreover, if we seek to discover the source of this tradition,
it soon becomes evident that we are touching upon one of the
earliest descriptions of the prophetic office as *nabi*. Far from being
a late, post-exilic projection of a shadowy figure, the office looms
up behind the traditions of the classical eighth-century prophets.
Both von Rad[58] and Würthwein[59] have emphasized the centrality
of the intercessary role of the early prophet. As the sacrifice was
constitutive for the office of the priest, so prayer was for the *nabi*.
He combined in one office the dual function of being Yahweh's
mouthpiece and Israel's representative before God. Through this
role he maintained the national well-being which was the *raison
d'être* of the office.

This office of prophetic intercessory appears as early as in the E
source in depicting Abraham's special position (Gen. 20.7ff.).
Much recent scholarly energy has been expended in discovering
its significance for the early kingdom and for the origins of the
classic prophets.[60] Especially in Deuteronomic circles the office
of *nabi* was continued. The law in Deut. 18.15ff. was an effort
to regulate the office and protect the nation against its abusers.[61]

[58] G. von Rad, 'Die falschen Propheten', *ZAW* 53 (1933), pp. 109ff.
[59] E. Würthwein, 'Amos-Studien', *ZAW* 62 (1950), pp. 1off.
[60] The literature is too vast to cite. Cf. the bibliographies in *IDB*, III, p.
919, and J. Muilenburg, 'The "office" of the Prophet in Ancient Israel', *The
Bible in Modern Scholarship*, ed. J. P. Hyatt (Nashville, 1965), pp. 74ff.
[61] von Rad, *op. cit.*, pp. 106f.

The Dtr. speech (I Sam. 12) depicts Samuel in this role as the interceding *nabi*, who comforts his people (v. 20) and intercedes for them. Likewise, Jeremiah who had been explicitly denied his role as intercessor (7.16) is approached by messengers from King Zedekiah with the request, 'pray for us to Yahweh our God' (37.3f.).

With this background in mind, the problem of interpreting II Kings 19 comes into sharper focus. The role of Isaiah in this chapter simply cannot be harmonized with his role in the poetic oracles. It is different in kind. The issue, however, is not between a genuinely historical picture and a non-genuine, but between two strikingly different portrayals, both of which make use of ancient traditions. The Dtr. redactor of II Kings 19 not only stood within a circle of tradition, but he made creative use of them to illustrate his own theology of history. Once again the author fused older and newer elements into a whole. The B^1 account of the Assyrian threat is brought to a close by the prophecy of retreat and ultimate destruction of the enemy. The fact that the death of Sennacherib occurred some twenty years after his return is lost in his scheme. The impression of the author's being at a considerable distance from the historical events of Sennacherib's death in 681 is not removed even by those who place much historical weight on the mention of Tirhakah.

We have criticized the wholesale dismissal of this chapter as later accretion of the pious legend. But equally misleading, and certainly more prevalent, is the attempt to gloss over the complexity of the problem of tradition and to blur the sharp contours of the different portrayals. The attempt to harmonize certain oracles of Isaiah with the prophetic activity in II Kings 19, and then to use this to buttress a historical theory of two invasions, suffers from basic methodological errors.[62]

To summarize: The analysis of the B^1 account has pointed out the highly complex nature of the traditions which make up the account. On the one hand, the study has shown a large layer of the material which reflects ancient tradition with a genuinely historical setting. On the other hand, we have seen also that newer elements have entered into the account and have been formed into a unified story which bears the stamp of the Dtr. author.

[62] Cf. John Bright, *A History of Israel*, pp. 74ff., 282ff., and G. Ernest Wright, *Isaiah* (London, 1964), pp. 18f.

D. ACCOUNT B² (II KINGS 19.9b-35 // ISA. 37.9b-36)⁶³

9b. Again he sent messengers to Hezekiah, saying, 10. 'Thus you shall speak to Hezekiah king of Judah: "Do not let your God in whom you trust deceive you by saying, Jerusalem will not be given into the hand of the king of Assyria. 11. Surely you have heard what the kings of Assyria have done to all lands, completely destroying them. And shall you be saved? 12. Have the gods of the nations delivered them, the nations which my fathers destroyed, Gozan, Haran, Rezeph, and the people of Eden who were in Tel-assar? 13. Where is the king of Hamath, the king of Arpad, the king of the city of Sepharvaim, the king of Hena, or the king of Ivvah?" '

14. Hezekiah took the letter from the hand of the messengers, and read it; and he went up to the house of Yahweh and spread it before Yahweh. 15. And Hezekiah prayed before Yahweh, and said: 'O Yahweh the God of Israel, who art enthroned above the cherubim, thou art God, even thou alone, over all the kingdoms of the earth; open thy eyes, O Yahweh, and see; and hear the words of Sennacherib, which he has sent to mock the living God. 17. Indeed, O Yahweh, the kings of Assyria have laid waste the nations and their lands, 18. and have cast their gods into the fire, for they were no gods, but the work of men's hands, wood and stone; therefore they were destroyed. 19. And now, O Yahweh our God, save us, I beseech thee, from his hand, that all the kingdoms of the earth may know that thou, O Yahweh, art God alone.'

20. Then Isaiah the son of Amoz sent to Hezekiah, saying, 'Thus says Yahweh, the God of Israel: Your prayer to me about Sennacherib king of Assyria (I have heard). 21. This is the word that Yahweh has spoken concerning him:

---

⁶³ Text criticism of II Kings 19.9b-35 // Isa. 37.9bff.: V. 11, Montgomery suggests changing the root to *ḥrb* as in v. 17 because Assyria did not practise the ban, but the emendation is not advisable. V. 14, critics follow the versions in reading consistently singular or plural. V. 15, Isa. *ṣĕbhā'ôth*. V. 16, read *šālaḥ* with Isa. V. 23, read *bĕrōbh* with Isa. and versions. Usually commentators have followed *BH* in reading waw cons., but this hardly solves the problem. Montgomery tries to maintain a distinction in tense. V. 25 *ûthĕhî* is extremely difficult. Montgomery follows AV in taking it as second person. V. 26, the final phrase is suspect and has evoked many suggested emendations. V. 27, the last half line seems to be a gloss taken from 28.

"She despises you, she scorns you—
   the virgin daughter of Zion;
She wags her head behind you—
   the daughter of Jerusalem.

22. Whom have you mocked and blasphemed?
   Against whom have you raised your eyes and haughtily lifted
     your eyes?
   Against the Holy One of Israel!

23. By your messengers/servants you have taunted Yahweh
   And said, 'With my many chariots I have gone up to the
     mountain tops to the far recesses of Lebanon,
   And cut down its tallest cedars, the choicest of its firs;
   And come to its farthest lodge/height, its densest forest.

24. It is I who have dug wells and drunk (foreign) waters,
   I who dried up with the soles of my feet all the streams of
     Egypt.'

25. Have you not heard that I determined it long ago?
   I planned from days of old what now I bring to pass,
   That you should be the one to turn fortified cities into heaps of
     ruins,

26. While their inhabitants, shorn of strength are dismayed and
     confounded,
   And become like plants of the field and like tender grass,
   Like grass on the housetops, and blasting before standing
     grain.

27. But I know your sitting down, and your going out and
   coming in, and your raging against me.

28. Because you have raged against me, and your arrogance has
   come into my ears,
   I will put my hook in your nose and my bit in your mouth,
   And I will turn you back on the way by which you came." '

29. 'And this shall be the sign for you: this year you shall eat the
after-growth, and in the second year what springs of the same;
then in the third year sow and reap, and plant vineyards, and eat
their fruit. 30. And the surviving remnant of the house of Judah
shall again take root downward and bear fruit upward; 31. For
out of Jerusalem shall go forth a remnant, and out of Mount Zion
a band of survivors. The zeal of Yahweh will do this.' 32. 'Therefore thus says Yahweh concerning the king of Assyria, "He shall
not come to this city or shoot an arrow there, or come before it

with a shield or cast a mound against it. 33. By the way that he came, by the same he shall return, and he shall not come into this city, says Yahweh, 34. for I will defend this city to save it, for my own sake, and for the sake of my servant David." '

35. And that night the angel of Yahweh went forth, and slew a hundred and eighty-five thousand in the camp of the Assyrians, and when men arose early in the morning, behold, these were all dead bodies.

An analysis of the structure of B^2 as a whole reveals a situation which is closely parallel to B^1. Again the passage consists of continuous narrative prose which joins together a series of speeches. The narrative portion, however, plays an even less significant role in B^2 than in B^1. Of the $26\frac{1}{2}$ verses which comprise the account, only three verses are taken up by the narrative (9b, 14, 21a, 35). It is of course to be considered that the narrative introduction has been greatly reduced by the combination of sources. Nevertheless, it is clear that the narrative commentary which provided the setting, and described the reactions of the participants in B^1 has been reduced to the minimum.

A more striking feature of B^2 emerges when one compares more closely the structure of the two accounts. In general, both contain the same pattern: the delivery of the message, the reaction of Hezekiah, the message from Yahweh, and the deliverance. However, the details vary considerably, both in content and amount of space alloted to each item. The initial delivery of the message by the Rabshakeh in B^1, first to the emissaries and then to the people, called for two long speeches. In B^2 this initial act has been compressed into one short speech of four verses. In place of Hezekiah's message to Isaiah in B^1, the king's prayer in B^2 is delivered to God directly and has been expanded to five verses. Finally, the message of Isaiah to Hezekiah, which occupied two verses in B^1, has been expanded to form more than half of the B^2 account.

This comparison, however, remains somewhat misleading unless one takes account of the secondary expansion within the B^2 account. It has long been noted that the message of Yahweh to Hezekiah through Isaiah which begins in v. 21 has been broken off and continued again in v. 33. The section which intervenes (vv. 22-32) quite clearly is an interpolation which has expanded the message of Yahweh greatly. The basic elements of the account remain the same without this expansion, but the original emphasis of B^2 comes clearer into focus without it. The whole account is then only half as long as B^1. This contraction of the material functions, however, to highlight the central features of the account which is now the king's prayer.

We turn next to examine each oracle separately. The message to Hezekiah from the Assyrians is introduced with the traditional formula which is directed to the messenger: 'So you shall say to Hezekiah, king of Judah.' The message then follows without the introductory formula of the message itself, 'thus says So and So', which was so prominent in B^1. Still there is a problem with the use of this instruction formula to the messengers in v. 10a. If the message is delivered orally according to the pattern of B^1, why was it necessary for Hezekiah to take the letter(s) from the messengers, read it, and spread it before Yahweh? While it is obvious from Near Eastern practice that the use of a letter does not exclude its oral delivery, the picture is not wholly consistent. The textual uncertainty in v. 10a has led some commentators to excise the phrase as secondary, but the confusion may have arisen from the Dtr.'s introduction of motifs from the B^1 account.

Many of the formal problems which were encountered in the diplomatic disputation oracles of B^1 are not present in B^2. The message to Hezekiah begins with an admonition which parallels somewhat vv. 29ff. in form. Then three questions which reinforce the one issue follow from different angles. Will you be saved from a fate different from that which befell all the other lands? Did the gods of the nations save them? What has happened to the kings of those cities which resisted? The oracle gives evidence of a higher degree of inner consistency than did its parallel. There are no abrupt changes in speakers,[64] nor sharp fluctuations in perspective. Once the central point has been made, the oracle ends abruptly. Indeed, the impression of contrived consistency has caused Procksch[65] to characterize the account as 'the legend of a saint, painted on a golden background, lifeless and distant from history'.

If we examine the content of the oracle, it is immediately

---

[64] The first person usage is consistent throughout. The third person reference to the king of Assyria in v. 10 is appropriate as a direct quotation of Yahweh.   [65] O. Procksch, *Jesaia I* (Leipzig, 1930), p. 452.

apparent that the grounds on which the whole argument rests differ from those of B¹. In the first account, the focus of the argument shifts continually as does the addressee. The Rabshakeh ridicules Egyptian help. He taunts the weakness of the defenders. When the speech turns to theology, the question is whether or not Yahweh's support can be counted on by Hezekiah. Has he not offended Yahweh and has not Yahweh ordered the attack on Jerusalem? Later on, Yahweh's power to save is attacked. But in the second account of B², all these issues are omitted except one. The entire controversy has been narrowed to the one all encompassing issue: Yahweh has made his promise to defend Jerusalem, but can he be trusted to sustain it? Everything has been subordinated to the one theological concern.

Of particular interest is the manner in which the author of B² has reworked his material. The first oracle parallels nearly sentence for sentence the phraseology of B¹, yet each time with a slight shift of meaning. 18.29 'do not let Hezekiah deceive you' is paralleled closely by 19.10a, 'do not let your God deceive you'. However, in B¹ the Rabshakeh is addressing the people, warning them against the promises of the king, while in B² the Assyrian is addressing the king, warning him against the promises of his God. Again, in B¹ the people are cautioned against believing the promise of Hezekiah: 'this city will not be given into the hand of the king of Assyria'. In B² it is Hezekiah who is cautioned against believing the same promise made to him by God (19.10). The same vocabulary of 'trust' and 'deliver' appears in both accounts (cf. 18.22 // 19.10; 18.30, 32 // 19.11) and the powerlessness of the foreign gods to save is illustrated in both. However, in B¹ it is Sennacherib who boasts of his past victories, whereas in B² the reference is to the victories of the former kings. Finally, in B¹ the Rabshakeh raises the ironical question, 'where are the gods of Hamath and Arpad . . .', while in B² the question has become 'where is the king of Hamath and Arpad?' . . .

Several points of interest emerge from the comparison. The close parallel in the language and syntax indicates clearly the large area of common ground shared by the two accounts. Yet the differences would tend to point to a body of tradition held in common rather than to a direct use of B¹ by B². The second account shows a limited selection of material. The parallels to B¹ occur, by and large, with the second speech of the Rabshakeh to the people.

The basic issue is the same: Do not trust in a promise of deliverance which goes against the hard facts of life. But in the first account Hezekiah is the deceiver; in the second it is Yahweh. In the first, the controversy involves the emissaries, the people, the king, and Isaiah. In the second, Hezekiah fights the battle of faith alone. In the first, a rich variety of historical references finds expression; in the second, the historical particulars recede into the background and emerge only in so far as they illustrate the type of the faithful king.

The prayer of Hezekiah (19.15-19) has no parallel in the B¹ account. It replaces the message of the king to Isaiah, requesting that the prophet pray to Yahweh on the remnant's behalf. The form of Hezekiah's prayer is strongly stamped by traditional cultic patterns, but over and above this, it is especially characteristic of the style of the Dtr. historian. Close parallels are found in II Sam. 7.18ff.; I Kings 8.22ff.; Jer. 32.16ff.; and in the later literature, II Chron. 20.5ff.; Neh. 9.6ff.; Dan. 9.3ff.; III Macc. 2.1ff.; 6.1ff. The basic structure of the prayer is that of the complaint psalm which combines the elements of invocation, complaint, and plea. In its Dtr. form the initial invocation is followed by an enumeration of the divine attributes in a style somewhat akin to the hymn. Yahweh is the 'God of Israel'; he 'dwells between the cherubim'; he 'alone is God of all the kingdoms of the earth'; he 'made heaven and earth'. The plea to attend, accompanied by reasons, leads into the complaint. The element of complaint which in the Psalter explicated in great detail the personal or national plight, has lost some of its intensity. Confidence in God's power has tempered the need. The supplicant is now equally as concerned over the honour of Yehweh which is being flaunted. The actual plea for intervention is introduced by 'and now'[66] (wĕ'attāh- v. 19; cf. I Kings 8.26; Neh. 9.32; II Chron. 20.10; Dan. 9.15) and closely followed by a motivation clause: 'that all . . . may know that thou art God alone.'

A glance at the content of the prayer reveals immediately all the classic elements of the Dtr. theology. Whereas in the B¹ account the mixture of old and new elements was a characteristic feature, the prayer of B² reflects consistently the same late per-

---

[66] Cf. A. Laurentin, 'We'attah- Kai nun', *Biblica* 45 (1964), pp. 168ff.; H. A. Brongers, 'Bemerkungen zum Gebrauch des Adverbialen We'attāh im Alten Testament', *VT* 15 (1965), pp. 289ff.

spective of the post-deuteronomic period. The central issue turns about the 'blasphemy of the living God'. The phrase occurred in B¹, but now it is in a thoroughly appropriate setting. Yahweh is contrasted in language which parallels Deutero-Isaiah (43.8ff.; 45.5ff.) with the 'no gods' of the nations which are only wood and stone. There can be no doubt that for this author Yahweh alone is God of heaven and earth. Typical for the Dtr. theology is the fusion of the old amphictyonic traditions of the pre-monarchial period with the traditions of the Jerusalem cult.⁶⁷ The God of the desert palladium (v. 15), creator of heaven and earth, ruler of all the kingdoms, promises to defend the city of David (v. 34). By his great act he makes himself known before the nations of the world.⁶⁸

Finally, the role of Hezekiah reflected in the prayer fits completely into the framework of Dtr.'s theology.⁶⁹ In B¹ Hezekiah's concern is to acquire the intercessory prayer of the prophet. However, in B² Hezekiah does not even inform Isaiah, but enters the temple, approaches the very presence of God, and offers as a royal priest the prayer of his people. Here the parallel with David (II Sam. 8.18), and Solomon (I Kings 8.14ff.) is striking. Hezekiah has become the type of the righteous king whose heart is perfect before God. The writer is already far removed from the Hezekiah of II Kings 18.13ff. The divine answer to the prayer of the king is given in vv. 20ff. As mentioned above, this answer has been interrupted by an interpolation in 21b-31. The break in continuity has necessitated a repetition of the messenger formula in 32 before a return to Yahweh's answer through his prophet. The message contains a promise, first stated negatively in terms of Assyria's impotency, and secondly, in positive terms concerning the divine protection of the city. As noticed earlier, v. 33 presents a problem in its present context and is probably a secondary harmonization.

The message of the prophet with its immediate fulfilment is closely attached to the preceding prayer. The prophet plays no independent role nor is his person significant. He is merely a

---

⁶⁷ von Rad, *Old Testament Theology*, I (Edinburgh and London, 1962), pp. 337ff.

⁶⁸ Cf. W. Zimmerli, *Erkenntnis Gottes nach dem Buche Ezechiel* (Zürich, 1954), pp. 27ff. for a study of this formula.

⁶⁹ Cf. the essay of H. W. Wolff, 'Das Kerygma des deuteronomistischen Geschichtswerk', *ZAW* 73 (1961), pp. 171ff., and von Rad, *op. cit.*, p. 345.

bearer of the divine message. The emphasis falls fully on the power of God in his word which then effects its task. The larger form is, therefore, not the prophetic legend which centres in the prophet's role such as I Kings 14 or II Kings 1, but a similar genre which focuses on a picture of the pious king. The account of Jehoshaphat in II Chron. 20 contains several additional elements, but it still reflects a parallel structure. There is the prayer, followed by the divine answer (in Chron. through a Levite), and finally the fulfilment (v. 24 'they were dead bodies on the ground; none had escaped'). The closeness of this form in the prophetic legend is shown by the continued role of the prophetic word which mediates the divine response. In the later form this element is lost, and God intervenes directly in response to the pious prayer (III Macc. 2.21; 6.18ff.). The powerful and moving style of the account is also characteristic of the early legend which form cannot be considered a sign of literary or theological decay in Israel by any means!

The attempt to fix the source of this legend of Sennacherib's destruction has evoked much discussion in the past without a consensus. In general, scholars have moved in two directions. Either, the legend is considered a creation out of whole cloth which is motived by wishful thinking. Then it is contrasted with the 'genuine' oracles of Isaiah (22.1ff.; 30.12ff.) which predict the destruction of Jerusalem (Marti, Meinhold, etc.). Or, the legend is thought to reflect a kernal of an historical tradition, held in common with the legend of Herodotus, which recalled a disastrous defeat of the Assyrian army in the vicinity of Egypt through a pestilence.[70] In our opinion, neither of these two alternatives are satisfactory. A more fruitful approach would be to search within Israel's traditions to see if there is material which might have formed the basis for the legend.

[70] The Herodotus account continues to be used by some American scholars to defend an 'historical kernal' theory. Cf. J. Bright, *A History of Israel*, p. 283; G. E. Wright, *Isaiah*, p. 82; S. H. Horn, *op. cit.*, p. 26. In the light of the tremendous problems associated with this legend, this procedure appears to me unjustified. Cf. the detailed treatment in Meinhold, *Die Jesajaerzählungen*, pp. 34ff.; W. Aly, *Volksmärchen, Sage und Novelle bei Herodot und seinen Zeitgenossen* (Göttingen, 1921); the collection of essays on Herodotus as a historian which is edited by W. Marg, *Herodot. Die Bemühungen um sein Verständnis* (*Wege der Forschung*, Band 26); and especially the careful evaluation with full bibliography of W. Baumgartner, 'Herodots Babylonische und Assyrische Nachrichten', *Zum Alten Testament und seiner Umwelt* (Leiden, 1959), pp. 305ff.

The closest linguistic parallel is found in Isa. 31.5, 8, which presents a number of difficulties of its own as we have seen earlier. V. 5 shares with II Kings the rather infrequent verb 'to defend' (*gnn*). The other parallels are conceptual rather than linguistic. Yahweh delivers Zion (Isa.-*hnṣl* || Kings *hwši*); he smites the Assyrians with the sword; the victory is without human aid. When one compares these motifs with other Isaianic oracles, particularly 14.24ff., the distance to a recognizable circle of Isaianic thought is not too great. Naturally there are many Isaianic motifs which are distinct and play no role, such as the deliverance by means of a theophany in Isa. 30.27, or the paradisiacal peace of 29.17ff. or 32.15ff.

The question arises whether there is any connection between the themes in the legend of II Kings and the Zion tradition which speaks of the destruction of the attacking enemy, 17.12ff.; 29.1-4; Ps. 46. Early in the Zion tradition the chaotic waters have been historicized to become the enemy. In both, Yahweh defends his city: 'he breaks the bow and shatters the spear.' In the Zion tradition the picture is of Yahweh dwelling in the city and repelling the attacks from without (Zech. 2.4f.). In both, the victory is sudden and without human assistance: 'in the morning they are no more.'

But equally important and decisive in evaluating the B[2] account, are the alterations which the traditional material underwent in its adaptation to the legend. First of all, the Zion tradition has received a new setting by its use in the legend which is strikingly different from its function in the cult or in the prophetic oracle. It is now given a fixed chronological position in Israel's history which involves the narrowing of a tradition which previously had oscillated freely between past and future. The enemy is likewise removed from its former position as the unidentified evil horde which occupied an undetermined place between heaven and earth, and has been identified with Sennacherib's army. The legend is not satisfied with the assurance of divine destruction of the enemy. It knows the exact manner of its execution (the angel of Yahweh with a sword), and the precise effect on the army (185,000 in number). Moreover, the motivation for the defence of the city is spelled out. It is for Yahweh's own sake and for the sake of David (I Kings 11.13, 34; II Kings 8. 19 etc.). Finally, and perhaps the most important distinction from the

Isaianic use of the tradition, the threat is directed not to haughty Assyria, but as a word of promise in response to the prayer of faithful Hezekiah.

The treatment of the two oracles which make up the interpolation in 21b-31 can be brief since this material is independent of the B² account both in form and content. The first oracle (21b-28) is a taunt song in poetic meter, directed against Assyria, which contains much old material. It is closely akin to Isa. 10.5ff. in its imitation of the bombastic style of the inscription (*Prunkinschrift*). Nevertheless, the theological framework in reference to Assyria (vv. 25ff.) is distinct from that of Isaiah, and remarkably close in language and thought to that of Deutero-Isaiah.

The second passage is a sign oracle whose original context is difficult to determine with any certainty. Its prediction that the normal operations of agriculture would be suspended for two harvests obviously removes it from the invasion setting of B². To the oracle has already been appended an eschatological interpretation (vv. 30f.) which is similar in tone to some of the post-exilic levels in Isaiah (4.2ff.).

The final question regarding the relation of the two accounts, B¹ and B², has, in large measure, already been answered indirectly. There is a common body of oral tradition shared by both accounts which appears in the similar structure of the stories and in the sections of parallel material. The many non-tendentious variations would rule out a literary relationship. However, the process through which the common material developed up to its final stage varied in the two sources. The work of the Dtr. redactor is evident in both accounts, but to a lesser degree in B¹. There is also some evidence for a mutual influencing of the two sources. It is possible for this blurring of lines to have been effected by the Dtr. redactor when he combined the sources or at an even later date.

To summarize: The analysis of the B² account has revealed the characteristics of this legendary source, and studied the effect which the genre has had on the presentation of the story. The effort to picture Hezekiah as the type of the faithful king has emerged as a dominant concern. The understanding that there is a radical alteration of traditional material which serves a new function for the author should provide a warning against a simple-minded historical reading of the text.

IV

THE CHRONICLER (II CHRONICLES 32)

1. After these things and this loyalty, Sennacherib the king of Assyria came and invaded Judah, and besieged the fortified cities, thinking to win them for himself. 2. When Hezekiah saw that Sennacherib had come and intended to fight against Jerusalem, 3. he consulted with his officers and leading men about closing up the springs that were outside the city, and they supported him. 4. A large number of people were brought together to stop up all the springs and the brook that flowed through the land, saying, 'Why should the kings of Assyria come and find abundant water?' 5. He went to work with determination and repaired every section of the wall which was damaged, erected towers upon it, and outside it he built another wall; and he strengthened the Millo in the city of David. He also made a large number of weapons and shields. 6. He set combat commanders over the people, and gathered them together to him in one square at the gate of the city and spoke encouragingly to them as follows: 7. 'Be strong and of good courage. Do not be afraid or dismayed before the king of Assyria and all the horde that is with him, for there is one greater with us than with him. 8. With him is an arm of flesh; but with us is Yahweh our God, to help us and to fight our battles.' And the people were reassured by the words of Hezekiah, king of Judah.

9. After this Sennacherib, king of Assyria, who was before Lachish with all his forces, sent his servants to Jerusalem to Hezekiah king of Judah and to all the people of Judah that were in Jerusalem saying, 10. 'Thus says Sennacherib king of Assyria, "On what are you relying that you stand siege in Jerusalem? 11. Is not Hezekiah deluding you that he may give you over to die by famine and thirst, when he tells you, 'Yahweh our God will save us from the hand of the king of Assyria'? 12. Is not Hezekiah the one who removed his high places and his altars and said to Judah and Jerusalem, 'Before one altar you shall worship, and upon it you shall burn your sacrifices'? 13. Do you not know what

I and my fathers have done to all the peoples of other lands? Were the gods of the nations of those lands at all able to deliver their lands out of my hand. 14. Who among all the gods of those nations which my fathers utterly destroyed was able to deliver his people from my hand, that your God should be able to deliver you from my hand? 15. Now, therefore, do not let Hezekiah deceive you or mislead you like this, and do not believe him, for no god of any nation or kingdom has been able to deliver his people from my hand or from the hand of my fathers. How much less will your God deliver you out of my hand!" '

16. And his servants spoke still more against Yahweh God and against his servant Hezekiah. 17. And he wrote letters to cast contempt on Yahweh the God of Israel and to speak against him, saying, 'Like the gods of the nations of the lands who have not delivered their people from my hands, so the God of Hezekiah will not deliver his people from my hand.' 18. And they shouted with a loud voice in the language of Judah to the people of Jerusalem who were upon the wall, to frighten and terrify them, in order that they might take the city. 19. And they spoke of the God of Jerusalem as they spoke of the gods of the peoples of the earth, which are the work of men's hands.

20. Then Hezekiah the king and Isaiah the prophet, the son of Amoz, prayed because of this and cried to heaven. 21. And Yahweh sent an angel, who cut off all the mighty warriors and commanders and officers in the camp of the king of Assyria. So he returned with shame of face to his own land. And when he came into the house of his god, his own offspring there struck him down with the sword. 22. Thus Yahweh saved Hezekiah and the inhabitants of Jerusalem from the hand of Sennacherib king of Assyria and from the hand of all his enemies, and he (gave them rest) on every side. 23. And many brought gifts to Yahweh at Jerusalem and costly presents to Hezekiah the king of Judah, so that he was exalted in the sight of all nations from that time onward.

The account of Sennacherib's invasion which is given by the Chronicler is of particular interest because of its singular relation to the parallels in the book of Kings. It is apparent that the Chronicler does not merely repeat the prior account, nor has he simply abbreviated his sources. Rather, a genuinely new literary creation has emerged which both shares much in common with Kings, and which also differs in important aspects.

Commentators have long since pointed out the obvious differences in the Chronicler's account. Whereas the Kings account presents the reform of Hezekiah in a few verses and sketches the invasion in great detail, the reverse is true in Chronicles. The reform occupies some three chapters and the actual invasion is condensed to half a chapter. The one account of Kings (A) speaks of a surrender; another of Hezekiah's great consternation and fear (B[1]). The Chronicler, however, portrays Hezekiah as a model of faith in God, who prepares resolutely to defend the city and who encourages his people in confidence against the vain human power of the enemy. The Chronicler's account gives evidence of many omissions. There is no reference to Egyptian help, nor to the other details of the Rabshakeh's disputation, nor to Isaianic oracles. Yet there is new material relating to the preparation which is over and above that of Kings, and which receives some historical confirmation by a similar reference in Isaiah (22.8ff.).

However, in spite of the many correct detailed observations in the commentaries, it remains a question whether the literary genre of the account has been adequately described. A basic characteristic of the account is its dependence upon written sources. This is not to suggest that the Chronicler's only source was Kings. The question of the scope and nature of other sources continues to be hotly debated. Rather, the point being argued is that the compiler of II Chron. 32 had the Kings account available to him as a written source.[1] The thesis of an alleged reference to temple records, which were independent of the book of Kings in its Dtr. redaction does not do justice to the Chronicler's text.[2] This dependence on a written source at once distinguishes the Chronicler's account from those of Kings. Both B[1] and B[2] were dependent on oral tradition which they then reworked in different ways. B[2] was classified as a legendary genre because its author recast the oral tradition into a form which was largely structured by a strong theological concern to edify. Although it is true that

---

[1] One of the most crucial questions for Chronicles remains the textual one importance of which has only recently been adequately recognized. Cf. Werner E. Lemke, 'The Synoptic Problem in the Chronicler's History', *HTR* 58 (1965), pp. 349ff. The broader implications on literary critical problems which Lemke draws are less convincing.

[2] Cf. M. Noth, *Überlieferungsgeschichtliche Studien*, I (Halle, 1943), pp. 131ff.

the Chronicler fashions his material into stereotyped patterns which reflect an ideal of piety like B², nevertheless, the classification of legend is inadequate to describe with precision the essential features of the Chronicler's account.

It is our thesis that the term 'midrash' is a much more appropriate description of the literary form.[3] By midrash we mean a specific form of literature which is the product of an exegetical activity by a circle of scholars in interpreting a sacred text. Essential to the midrash is its attempt to elucidate a written source. This process functions in terms of a dialectic movement which proceeds from the interpreter to the text, and *vice versa*, from the text to the interpreter. On the one hand, the form of the midrash is structured by a serious wrestling with the problems arising from the text itself. On the other hand, categories of interpretation which are independent of the text in origin are brought to bear upon it. The term midrash is basically misunderstood when it is employed in a derogatory fashion to designate a literature which is very loosely related in a tendentious manner to an historical account.[4] We are suggesting that the literary form of this chapter of the Chronicler can best be described in reference to this exegetical activity by a circle of interpreters.

First, we shall examine the account, for examples, which reveal an attempt to come to terms with a problem or condition in the text. II Chron. 32.9 reads: 'Sennacherib sent his servants to Jerusalem to Hezekiah while he was besieging (*hû' 'al*) Lachish with all his forces.' The circumstantial clause in 9ab describes the existing state of the Lachish siege at the time of the dispatching of

---

[3] L. Zunz's treatment remains classic, *Die gottesdienstlichen Vorträge der Juden*² (Frankfort, 1892), pp. 37ff. Cf. the excellent articles with bibliography by Horovitz and Theodor in the *JE*, vol. VIII. The following are significant recent discussions of midrashic method: R. Bloch, 'Midrash', *Suppl. au Dict. de la Bible*, V, pp. 1263ff.; I. L. Seeligmann, 'Voraussetzungen der Midraschexegese', *Suppl. VT*, I (1953), pp. 150ff.; J. Goldin, *The Living Talmud* (New York, 1957); G. Vermes, *Scripture and Tradition in Judaism* (Leiden, 1961); A. G. Wright, 'The Literary Genre Midrash', *CBQ* 28 (1966), pp. 105ff.

[4] J. Wellhausen's characterization is a misunderstanding which has wrought much havoc, *Prolegomena to the History of Israel* (Edinburgh, 1885), p. 227: 'Midrash is the consequence of the conservation of all the relics of antiquity, a wholly peculiar artificial reawakening of dry bones, especially by literary means. . . . Like ivy it overspreads the dead trunk with extraneous life, blending old and new in a strange combination . . . but in the process it is twisted and perverted, and set off with foreign accretions in the most arbitrary way.'

an envoy to Jerusalem. A comparison of the Chronicler's statement with his sources is illuminating. Mention of Lachish occurs
three times in the Kings accounts. In II Kings 18.14 Hezekiah
sent his message of capitulation to Sennacherib who was at
Lachish. In 18.17 the Rabshakeh left Lachish with a great army for
Jerusalem. In 19.8 he departed for Libnah 'for he heard that the
king had left Lachish'. None of these verses establish the exact
relation between the siege of Lachish and the envoy to Jerusalem.
18.14 merely states that Lachish served as the Assyrian head-
quarters. The city might have been taken months before. V. 13
mentions his taking 'all the fortified cities of Judah'. Historically
speaking, the exact chronological sequence of the Assyrian
campaign is unclear, particularly since the Assyrian annal at times
is topically arranged.[5] It seems evident that the Chronicler has no
new sources at hand, but has deduced this sequence from his
Kings sources. If the Assyrians were at Lachish when the envoy
was first sent, and then departed to attack Libnah, he assumes,
not only that Lachish had fallen, but that it had been immediately
under siege. In this case, the Chronicler has not attempted to
resolve a discrepancy in his sources, but has made explicit a point
of previous chronological uncertainty by reasoning from them.

There are several examples in Chronicles which go beyond
merely summarizing the two accounts into one; they also attempt
to harmonize a complexity in the text. So, for example, in II Kings
19.3ff. (B[1]) Hezekiah is reticent to pray directly and requests
Isaiah to pray on his behalf. In 19.14ff (B[2]) Hezekiah confidently
offers a lengthy prayer with no reference to Isaiah's intercession.
The Chronicler harmonizes the difficulty by having both Hezekiah
and Isaiah pray (32.20). Again, in B[1] Sennacherib points out the
fate of the nations and boasts, 'Who among all the gods of the
countries have delivered their countries out of *my* hand' (18.35).
In B[2] the parallel message reads, 'Have the gods of the nations
delivered them, the nations which *my fathers* destroyed' (19.12)?
The Chronicler resolves the tension by making reference to both:
'that *I* and my fathers have done' (32.13).

Again, in 18.17ff. the message of the Assyrian king is addressed
to Hezekiah as one would expect, but later the Rabshakeh
exploits the situation to harangue the people directly (18.26ff.).
The Chronicler combines the accounts by having the message

[5] Cf. the discussion in H. Haag, *op. cit.*, pp. 355f.

directed at the outset to both the king and the people (32.10). Finally, the two accounts of the giving of the message in B¹ and B² stand juxtaposed without any inner relation. The Chronicler makes reference both to the speech of B¹ and to the letter of B², yet he does it in such a way as to establish in a creative way a new relation between them. The reference to the letter (32.17) is placed in between the actual speech (32.10-15) and the shouting to the people on the wall (32.18). It has thus been subordinated to function as another illustration of the same blasphemous conduct which was evidenced in the speech. The Chronicler, by omitting the object of the shouting, changes the original function of the shouting and makes it serve as a means of terror.

There is one more example which illustrates the Chronicler's close attention to his sources and his creative attempt to alleviate a difficulty. In II Kings 18.17 the Rabshakeh is accompanied to Jerusalem by 'a large army', while Sennacherib remained at Lachish. In 19.8 the Rabshakeh returns from Jerusalem to Libnah, but there is no explicit reference to the army. Now if one disregards the modern critical theories of sources and reads the text consecutively as the Chronicler would have done, then there is the possibility that the army remained besieging Jerusalem. The sign in vv. 29-31, if it were in the text by this time, would support the idea of a continuous siege, as would also the emphasis on Yahweh's defence of the city against attack (vv. 32-34). Therefore, it is quite possible to connect the destruction of the hundred and eighty-five thousand in 19.35 with the great army of 18.17 which was encamped around Jerusalem. Montgomery, in fact, makes this same connection.

Surprisingly enough, the Chronicler does not accept this interpretation; rather, he makes it clear that the army remained at Lachish and only a group of envoys communicated the message to Hezekiah in Jerusalem. He is then completely logical in making clear that the destruction of the enemy was at Lachish. By specifying 'the camp of the king of Assyria' rather than merely the 'Assyrian camp' of II Kings 19.35 he removes the geographical ambiguity of the earlier account. There is no reason to believe that the Chronicler was dependent on some independent source of tradition for this interpretation. Rather, the evidence points to an exegetical technique which arose from a close study of the prior sources.

Now it is necessary to examine the other movement in the midrash which brings to the text a set of categories which do not stem from the text itself. These are the elements in Chronicles which are usually pointed out by the critical commentators; however, it is important to see them in conjunction with the full dialectic of the midrashic method. Right from the start it is clear that the Chronicler is concerned to fashion his sources in such a way that Hezekiah appears in the most favourable light. He has no interest in the exact date of Sennacherib's invasion which was given in Kings, but he begins by setting the attack to follow the 'faithful acts' of the temple reform. In fact, the Chronicler can make no use whatever of the A account's report of Hezekiah's surrender and even modifies Sennacherib's capture of the fortified cities to appear as merely his intention (v. 2). The preparation for the attack is described in terms which have no parallel in Kings, and the tradition would seem to be a genuinely historical one. Significantly, this action which was condemned in Isa. 22 as disbelief, is given a fully positive interpretation by the Chronicler. In his speech of encouragement Hezekiah formulates programatically the issue at stake: the basic question is faith in Yahweh.[6] All the political and military issues which still are reflected in B¹ have disappeared. This tendency is most evident in the actual speech. The Chronicler goes even beyond B² in making the issue completely a theological one. The constant repetition of the verb 'not able' (vv. 13, 14) emphasizes the point. The Chronicler does not allow the enemy for a moment to play Hezekiah off against Yahweh as B² had pictured. Their positions are identical throughout and the issue of faith is clear cut between God with his servant Hezekiah and the Assyrian threat. By a slight change in syntax the argument of the Rabshakeh concerning the removal of Yahweh's altars is redirected. In Kings the suggestion is made that Yahweh has been insulted and therefore will not help Israel. In Chronicles the reform is used by the enemy to show that Hezekiah cannot be trusted. Naturally for the reader the effect is just the opposite since he has been taught to value the reform as Hezekiah's greatest act of faithfulness.

In the summary the theological issue is again stated (vv. 17ff.). The blasphemy tradition has developed far beyond the Kings

---

[6] G. von Rad, *Das Geschichtsbild des chronistischen Werkes* (Stuttgart, 1930), pp. 16f.; A. C. Welch, *The Work of the Chronicler* (London, 1939), pp. 100f.

account toward its most extreme form in Daniel. The Assyrians 'cast contempt on Yahweh', 'speak against him', and worst of all, identify 'the God of Jerusalem'[7] with the no-gods of the nations (v. 19). It is a typical pattern of the Chronicler for the prayer of the righteous to evoke an immediate and direct response from God without a prophetic promise or sign (cf. II Chron. 14.11; 20.5ff.). The agent of the judgment on the Assyrians is no longer the 'messenger of Yahweh', but an angel, which reflects Israel's developing angelology in the post-exilic period.

It seems also to be a characteristic pattern of the account that the issue of deliverance revolves about Yahweh's rescue of 'his people' (vv. 10-15). The centrality of the city of Jerusalem which occurs repeatedly in Kings recedes and is replaced by its inhabitants. This is not to imply that the concern for Jerusalem has been neglected (cf. v. 19), but rather to illustrate concern for the deliverance of the nation which would be understandable in the post-exilic period. The final reference to Hezekiah's exaltation, particularly before the nations, brings the account to a conclusion.

To summarize: The Chronicler's account of the invasion of Sennacherib is midrashic in form. It arises from an attempt to interpret the written sources of Kings. The author's method shows, on the one hand, great attention to the details of the text which he often reinterprets with insight, but, on the other hand, the use of a set of principles, formulated independently of the text, which largely determine the nature of the interpretation.

[7] Cf. Th. C. Vriezen, *Jahwe en zijn Stad* (Amsterdam, 1962), pp. 4f. on the expression.

1. Woe to you, destroyer, who yourself have not been destroyed;
   You treacherous one, with whom none has dealt treacherously!
   When you have ceased to destroy, you will be destroyed,
   And when you have made an end of treachery, you will be dealt
     with treacherously.
2. O Yahweh, be gracious to us; we wait for thee.
   Be (our arm) every morning, our salvation in time of trouble.
3. At the noise of a tumult peoples flee,
   When thou liftest thyself up the nations are scattered;
4. And spoil is gathered (as the locust) gathers;
   They will swarm upon it as grasshoppers swarm.
5. Yahweh is exalted, for he dwells on high,
   He fills Zion with justice and righteousness;
6. And he will be the stability of your times,
   Abundance of salvation, wisdom and knowledge,
   The fear of Yahweh is his treasure.
7. Behold, the (men of Ariel) cry without,
   The messengers of (Salem) weep bitterly;
8. The highways have been made desolate, the wayfarer has ceased.
   Covenants are broken, (witnesses) are despised,
   There is no regard for man.
9. The land mourns and languishes;
   Lebanon is confounded and withers away;
   Sharon is like a desert; and Bashan and Carmel shake off their leaves.
10. 'Now I will arise,' says Yahweh.
    'Now I will lift myself up; now I will be exalted.
11. You conceive chaff, you bring forth stubble;
    (My) breath is a fire that will consume you.

[1] Text criticism of Isa. 33: Parentheses in the translation indicate emendations. V. 1, *kannĕlōthĕkhā* is a doubtful *hapax* which is usually emended. V. 2, reads with some versions and *BH* *zĕrō'ēnû*. V. 4, the conjecture *šalāl kĕmô* eases the difficulty. V. 6a, the sense is doubtful and is therefore often emended. V. 7, *'er'ellām* remains a difficult crux. The accepted emendation seems to be the best solution up to now. Read also 'Salem'. V. 8, read *'ēdhîm*. V. 11, emend with *BH*. V. 17, Gunkel and other emend here unnecessarily. V. 21a, the text is certainly corrupt, but no consensus has emerged. Some emend *'addîr* into a verbal form: Yahweh will be glorified. Others read *yĕ'ōr* (river). *BH* follows Duhm in reading *'ăphîq* (stream). The exact sense of the verse is not clear. V. 23, read *yĕḥallēq 'iwwēr* with Duhm, Gunkel, *BH*.

12. And the peoples will be burnt like lime,
    Like thorns cut down, that are burnt with fire.'
13. Hear, you who are far off, what I have done;
    And you who are near, acknowledge my might.
14. The sinners in Zion are afraid; trembling has seized the impious.
    'Who among us can dwell with the devouring fire?
    Who among us can dwell with eternal flames?'
15. He who walks righteously and speaks uprightly;
    He who despises the gain of oppressions,
    Who shakes his hands lest they hold a bribe,
    Who stops his ears from hearing of bloodshed,
    And shuts his eyes from looking upon evil.
16. He will dwell on the heights;
    His place of defence will be the fortresses of rocks;
    His bread will be given him, his water will be sure.
17. Your eyes will see the king in his beauty;
    They will behold a land that stretches afar.
18. Your mind will muse on the terror:
    'Where is he who counted? Where is he who weighed?
    Where is he who counted the towers?'
19. You will see no more the savage people,
    The people of an obscure speech which you cannot comprehend.
    Stammering in a tongue which you cannot understand.
20. Look upon Zion, the city of our appointed feasts.
    Your eyes will see Jerusalem, a quiet habitation, an immovable tent,
    Whose stakes will never be plucked up, nor any of its cords broken.
21. But there Yahweh in majesty will be for us
    A place of broad rivers and streams,
    Where no galley with oars can go, nor stately ship pass.
22. For Yahweh is our judge, Yahweh is our ruler, Yahweh is our king;
    He will save us.
23. Your tackle hangs loose; they shall not fix the mast,
    Or keep the sail spread out.
    Then will the (blind share) spoil in abundance,
    And the lame will seize the booty.
24. And no inhabitant will say, 'I am sick';
    The people who dwell there will be forgiven their iniquity.

The fundamental literary analysis of Isa. 33 was carried through in 1924 by H. Gunkel.[2] Since this study almost nothing new has emerged, and certainly nothing to modify significantly Gunkel's major thesis.[3] The earlier literary critical work of Stade[4] and

---

[2] H. Gunkel, 'Jesaia 33, eine prophetische Liturgie', *ZAW* 42 (1924), pp. 177ff.

[3] Fohrer's attempt, *Das Buch Jesaja*, II, *ad loc.*, to isolate two oracles in the chapter does not commend itself.

[4] B. Stade, *ZAW* 4 (1884), pp. 260ff.

Cheyne[5] had already shown convincingly why the chapter must be post-exilic, rather than being a contemporary prophetic report on the Assyrian invasion. However, the literary critics had been unable to decide on a context, and searched wildly for historical allusions in the Persian, Greek, and Maccabean eras. Mowinckel's[6] suggestion of a cultic setting had pointed in the right direction, but without the needed precision to convince. Gunkel's thesis of a prophetic liturgy was able for the first time to take account of the great variety of literary forms within the one oracle (woe oracle, national lament, prophetic oracle, Torah liturgy), and to establish the function of the oracle within the cultic life of the community. The oracle presupposes the desolation of Jerusalem, and awaits the restoration of Zion with expectancy, when the oppressor would be destroyed, Jerusalem freed of sinners, and the new Zion established under the kingship of Yahweh. The liturgy oscillates abruptly between momentary reflection on the dismal past, fervent prayers of the present worshippers, and elaborate sketches of the coming deliverance.

Our interest in this chapter is aroused because it shows a situation in which a later, prophetic tradition continued to reflect on the events of 701. Moving in its own peculiar circles it fashioned out of the older material a new pattern. Apparently this process was complex. On the one hand, the events of the Assyrian invasion exercised a discernible impact in shaping the prophetic tradition of Isa. 33. New forces were unleashed by this incident into the stream of Israel's tradition which left distinctive marks in their wake. Yet on the other hand, the traditions transmitted by the liturgy exercised a powerful pressure in shaping the understanding of the events of 701. The form and content of Israel's prior tradition did much to provide the context of understanding for the later community. Because these two movements are intricably entwined, and because the direction of the mutual influences cannot always be determined, it seems wise to treat them together.

The oracle begins in the traditional form of the woe oracle, directed against the nations. The enemy is not named, but poignantly characterized: the destroyer, yet himself not destroyed! In later prophecy similar phrases become common in describing the fate of the oppressor (Isa. 21.2; 24.16; Jer. 51.24; Ezek.

[5] T. K. Cheyne, *Introduction to the Book of Isaiah* (London, 1895), pp. 163ff.
[6] S. Mowinckel, *Psalmenstudien*, II (Kristiania, 1922), pp. 235ff.

25.15f.; 38.10; Hab. 2.8). Although this succinct formula does not occur in the primary oracles of Isaiah, the close connection in the content with Isaiah's threat against Assyria seems clear. Assyria is the rod of Yahweh who spoils and plunders, but who will herself one day be cut off (10.5ff.). The later gloss in v. 12 spells out explicitly the sequence and offers a close parallel to 33.1. The Isaianic scheme for understanding the role of Assyria has become a typical pattern for Israel's enemy *par excellence*. Israel has been devastated, but awaits the moment when the tables will be turned against the oppressor. The theme of the treachery of the enemy which recurs at times in the later enemy tradition (Isa. 21.2; 24.16; Hab. 1.13) is not specifically Isaianic in origin, but is common in the psalmist's complaints to characterize the wicked (25.3, etc.). Israel's enemy is further pictured as speaking an obscure, foreign language. A similar reference appears in Jer. 5.15 in reference to the enemy-from-the-north, but in general, this theme did not become an element in the stereotyped picture of the enemy. Rather, it seems directly related to the Assyrian invasion and the significant role which the language played in the poetic and narrative traditions (Isa. 28.11; 36.11ff.).

The description of Israel's plight (vv. 7ff.) is a complex mixture of older and newer elements. If the emendation of Ariel and Salem in v. 7 is correct, then the connection with Isaiah's role is a rather close one (29.1ff.). The ancient Zion tradition of the enemy attacking the city has been modified. Jerusalem is not only threatened, but suffers devastation and is in great straits. However, the actual description of her suffering lacks all historical specificity. The parallels with the song of Deborah (Judg. 5.6ff.) have long been noticed, and the land which is described is not Judah, but Lebanon and East Jordan. The older attempt to see in the reference to a broken covenant (v. 8) some perfidious act of Sennacherib is out of the question. Duhm with his characteristic pungency observes that it was Hezekiah and not Sennacherib who broke the treaty![7]

The manner in which the deliverance is sought and obtained follows completely the lines which have been set by the tradition. The prayer of petition is the fixed form of the community lament. The cultic setting separates it completely from the historical role attributed to Hezekiah as mediator, in spite of the fact that the

[7] Duhm, *op. cit.*, p. 217.

broad pattern of threat, plea, and deliverance is shared with the narrative account of Kings. Yahweh's intervention is described in the well-known theophanic idiom: he arises, his breath is a consuming fire, the thunderous nations flee in panic. The destruction is sudden and Israel is left reflecting on a terror which has no power (Isa. 17.14). Along with the judgment directed against the enemy, is the fear which it generated among the sinful within Israel. The form of this inner purging is the Torah liturgy (cf. Pss. 15; 24; Micah. 6.6ff., etc.). Certainly this restricting of the divine judgment of Israel to the wicked is far removed in spirit from the radical comprehensiveness of Isaiah's threat which encompassed the whole nation.[8] Nevertheless, the fact of inner judgment preceding deliverance is a prophetic note which was not present in the ancient Zion tradition and indicates an alteration which becomes characteristic of the post-exilic age.

The picture of the future salvation of Israel takes up into the prophetic eschatology many of the ancient motifs of the Zion paradise tradition. Jerusalem has been transformed into Zion, the inviolable, immovable habitation of the righteous. Zion becomes a place of healing streams where there are no sick and ailing. Yahweh rules as king and judge over his people.

This analysis illustrates well the characteristic manner by which Israel reflected on her past. The impact of the Assyrian invasion on the growing tradition can be clearly discerned in this oracle. It has left its stamp both on the content and form of the material. Older motifs have been formed into a new constellation, and newer elements have been introduced which continue in a stable form throughout the ensuing period. Still the reverse process is equally at work. Particularly, cultic tradition has provided a framework into which the past is understood. A new context has been provided in which the past event serves a new function. The Assyrian crisis has become a type of a recurrent threat. The need has been incorporated into a liturgical celebration which is ongoing. The deliverance has been placed within the eschatological framework of prophetic hope.

The study of Isa. 33 is important because it illustrates with great clarity one direction in which the tradition developed. It is now appropriate to return to a topic which was discussed in an earlier chapter and to draw some connections. The study of the

[8] H. W. Wolff, *Das Zitat im Prophetenspruch* (München, 1937), pp. 66ff.

oracle of promise in Isaiah (ch. II C) revealed that the great majority of promise oracles did not belong to the primary level of Isaianic tradition. Rather, passages such as 10.20-27; 29.17-21; 30.18-26; 32.15-20 were a secondary development. A closer examination of these passages shows immediately that this development is closely akin to that which we find in Isa. 33, in fact, it belongs to the same circle of tradition.

The pattern of Isa. 33 is closely paralleled in this set of promise oracles although often the full scope of the pattern is lacking. Israel is a people, destroyed and smitten (10.20, 24; 30.20). For a brief moment Yahweh has allowed the enemy to punish (10.25; 29.17). Soon he will again be gracious (30.19). He will appear in a mighty theophany (29.6) and destroy both the enemy and the wicked within (10.22f., 25; 29.20; 30.19). Then paradise will return to Zion (29.17; 30.23ff.; 32.15). The blind will see; the deaf will hear, and all sorrow will vanish (29.18; 30.19-26). Yahweh will rule his safe habitation in justice and peace for ever (32.16f.).

In summary: The analysis of ch. 33 shows an important and widespread development within Israel which continued to reflect on the Assyrian threat. It refashioned the tradition within a cultic framework of prophetic eschatology and altered the context of the original crisis to suit a later and different situation.

VI

HISTORICAL AND THEOLOGICAL
CONCLUSIONS

A. THE HISTORICAL PROBLEM

THIS study of the Assyrian crisis in Israel's history began with a recognition that an impasse had been reached. No one theory of how to reconstruct the events of 701 had been able to win widespread acceptance. Each approach had certain features which served to illuminate the fragmentary sources through a particular combination, but similarly each suffered from an inability to do full justice to all the material. The concern of this monograph was not to offer another reconstruction with the hope of overcoming some of the difficulties of the existing theories. Without some new sources, or a very new handling of the known material, such an enterprise seems fruitless. Therefore, this study attempted to determine the exact nature of the biblical sources with a greater precision than had been apparent in previous work. The method employed was a form critical analysis of the traditions relating to the Assyrian crisis. It was the hope that such an analysis would serve to clarify the nature of the impasse, and perhaps even contribute to its resolution.

The results of our study in reference to the historical problem have been mainly negative. The clarity which was achieved in describing the sources often served to eliminate several of the previous suggested solutions as highly improbable. The complex nature of the development of the multiple traditions served to intensify the historical problems rather than to alleviate the difficulties. What has become abundantly clear is the use to which historical situations have been put within the various biblical sources often renders them extremely inarticulate for the particular concerns of the modern historian.

The complex nature of the tradition underlying the biblical sources has made certain of the traditional historical solutions suspect. First of all, the frequent attempt to build a reconstruction on a combination of selected incidents taken uncritically from sources A and B (II Kings 18.13-16; II Kings 18.17ff.) is methodologically unsound. The effect on the formulation of these texts of traditions which were transmitted in a variety of ways to execute different functions within changing contexts cannot be dismissed by a simplistic combination of isolated events. The theory of a succession of events leading from the initial capitulation in source A to the subsequent victory in B has been confused in supposing that the final form of the biblical redaction corresponds to the historical sequence. An examination of the pre-literary stages does not support the same sequence and reveals its historical artificiality.

In a similar way, the two invasions theory has dealt with sources A and B on the one level, and tried to relate each source to a corresponding historical event. This manoeuvre has failed to note that many of the forces which shaped the B accounts were not historical events. We were able to isolate diverse influences such as the patterns of the Zion tradition, the Dtr. understanding of the prophetic office, and the literary fusion of sources. A study of these factors has buttressed the position that the diverse approaches to the Assyrian crisis arose from an involved traditional development, and not from different historical events. Bright's[1] defence of the two invasion theory is a classic example of a method which cross examines its sources on a flat level without recognizing either the pre-history of the sources or the totally different contexts in which the traditions functioned.

Secondly, our form critical analysis has critical implications for the theory which holds genuinely historical tradition to be only in the A account, and discounts the other narrative sources as unreliable. First, one cannot support the broad use of the category 'legend' to encompass all the material in B[1] and B[2], such as one finds in Rudolph.[2] Our analysis has shown significant differences in the form and traditions of B[1] and B[2]. Moreover, the B[1] account reflects a level of very ancient tradition which corresponds to contemporary Assyrian practice, and cannot be cavalierly dismissed as the literary product of a ripe imagination. The problem of how these traditions relate historically to those of the A account remains unsolved, yet the need is acute to deal critically with the full range of existing traditions.

[1] J. Bright, *A History of Israel*, pp. 282ff.
[2] W. Rudolph, *op. cit.*, p. 74.

Again, this study does not support the attempt[3] to treat the B accounts as simply a later influencing of the Zion traditions on the interpretation of the Assyrian crisis in which the historical events were fully absorbed into the traditional pattern of attack and deliverance. The role of the Zion tradition, which is only one among many, is complex and varied. It appeared in the primary level of the Isaianic oracles with important alteration, and certainly became a dominant force in the later post-exilic era. However, its influence in structuring the B[1] tradition must not be over-emphasized.

Finally, those theories which have attempted an easy correlation between Isaiah's oracles and certain portions of the narrative accounts have, almost without exception, been guilty of over-simplification. The oracles of Isaiah are far too complex and diversified to allow for a simple formulation of his position on Assyria which could then serve as a criterion for measuring the historical elements in the narrative material. The so-called 'Isaiah of legend' is not so easily disentangled from the alleged 'historical Isaiah'.

Even more seriously at fault is the attempt to understand the polarity of Isaiah's thought by means of an historical reconstruction of a two invasion theory. An alleged historical distinction is found in the narrative section—Isaiah pronounced Israel's judgment on the first invasion, but held out promise for the second—which is then made the measuring rod for structuring the oracles of Isaiah into corresponding parts.[4] Not only does this obliterate the distinctions of literary genres, but it eliminates the need for an accurate fixing of a context from the oracle itself. Such a method not only confuses the historical issues, but prevents an appreciation of Isaiah's message.

In conclusion: The historical problems have not been solved; in fact, greater complexity calls for even greater caution. The form critical analysis has offered aid to the historian in his ongoing task by distinguishing the various kinds of sources which are present in the Old Testament. In terms of the specific historical problem of 701, it seems unlikely that a satisfactory historical solution will be forthcoming without fresh extra-biblical evidence.

[3] G. von Rad, *Old Testament Theology*, II, pp. 155ff.
[4] Bright, *op. cit.*, p. 286; G. E. Wright, *Isaiah*, pp. 17ff.

B. THE THEOLOGICAL PROBLEM

The largely negative results of our historical conclusions are a warning against trying to understand these texts exclusively from an historical point of view. We have seen the extent to which the texts simply do not lend themselves to answering this set of questions. Also this predominant historical interest has obscured the understanding of the manner in which the texts themselves really function. The literary analysis has clarified the great variety of response to this cluster of historical events. It pointed out the effect of prior tradition on the structuring of the reaction, of the indirect influence of various responses upon each other, and of the shifting contexts into which the speakers and writers addressed their message.

It is not our contention that this is an unusual problem which is peculiar only to this group of texts. In principle, most portions of the Bible are involved to some degree with a similar exegetical issue. Naturally the intensity of the problem varies greatly. The texts related to the Assyrian crisis are of particular interest because of the large number of differing responses and because of the clarity with which the various forms have emerged. At least six distinct genres have been isolated and described which have reference to a related subject: the prophetic oracles of Isaiah, the annalistic type report (A), the Dtr. redaction of historical tradition (B[1]), the legend of the righteous king (B[2]), the midrash of the Chronicler, and the prophetic, eschatological liturgy (Isa 33). The primary theological problem turns on the issue of how one seeks to understand and evaluate this diversity of witness.

The case has been made with great persuasiveness by James Barr[5] against the common tack of using the action of God in history as the principal organizing bracket by which to unify the diversity. In terms of the example under scrutiny, it is not possible to see the diversity as human interpretations of the one selfsame action of God in history. The relation of these texts to the historical events and to each other is of a far more complex nature. There is no historical nucleus to which all the interpretations relate. The plotting of varying contexts does not reveal any common angle of vision from which the images are refracted. If one chooses to speak of the process of Israel's tradition building as 'history', then the semantic range of the term has broadened to

[5] James Barr, *Old and New in Interpretation* (London, 1966), pp. 15ff.

such an extent as to be unrecognizable by its original defenders. Moreover, the polarity of the action of God in the historical event and the human response in interpretation finds no basis whatever in the texts which have been analysed. Particularly embarrassing for such an approach is the inability to establish with any degree of historical certainty what this one act was to which Israel allegedly responded.

Barr has proposed the substitution of the term 'situation' in the place of the phrase 'acts of God in history'. The suggestion has much to commend it both for its freedom from overtones for most biblical scholars,[6] as well as for its modest claims. Still it remains a question of how much ground is permanently won when the term requires further refinement to make room for such essential elements of the biblical situation as its cumulative character. And could not other constitutive elements be added? While Barr is undoubtedly right in questioning the stake which the 'God who acts' position has in relating each situation to historical events, does it not belong somehow to the task of understanding the situation to determine in each case the degree of historical relatedness? Some situations are controlled by historical elements; others remain relatively or completely free from such. However, it belongs to the descriptive task to understand what forces are operative on a given text.

What seems essential is that the interpreter recognize the interaction in every context—and I prefer this to situation—between the stimulus which calls forth the response and the response which affects the stimulus. A context can be shaped by a situation, but at the same time, exercise a force which affects the situation. In the case of B^1, the Assyrian crisis produced a response in a circle of tradition which finally entered the Dtr. history. However, the traditional patterns of these circles exercised an enormous role in selecting and colouring the response. A recognition of this two way movement prevents one from sharply separating fact from interpretation. Equally important, it points up the opposite danger of supposing that one meaning is somehow built into the facts apart from a given context.[7] If this were the case, the mean-

[6] It remains unclear to me to what extent Barr has been influenced in his choice of the term by P. Tillich, *Systematic Theology* I (Chicago, 1951 and London, 1953), pp. 3ff.

[7] Cf. J. R. Lucas, 'On Not Worshipping Facts', *Philosophical Quarterly* 8

ing could be determined apart from its function in a given context. Much of the difficulty which interpreters of Scripture encounter in understanding the multiple directions found in the biblical witness arises from a presupposition that one correct meaning should adhere to each event, and any divergence is therefore a distortion.

Our study has shown how the changing contexts in which texts related to the Assyrian crisis functioned within the Old Testament. There was a closeness to the historical sequence of events in the A account, appropriate to the use of an annal, which was not present in the legendary form of B². Again, the effect of the Chronicler's reflecting on the Assyrian crisis by means of written texts afforded a totally different setting from the liturgical use of the traditional material by the community. Or again, the form critical analysis of Isaiah's oracles revealed that his message assumed both variety in form and content, depending on the particular setting in which they were given. The fact that contexts and usage vary only becomes an insurmountable problem when fluctuation is conceived of as inconsistency because it is measured by some alleged doctrine of Zion's inviolability which has been attributed to the prophet.

One of the most consistent theological problems which arises in connection with biblical diversity is the application of norms for establishing some order of relative value among the many testimonies. It should not be denied that an interpreter of a text is often called upon to make value judgments. In the analysis of the historical problem under consideration we were forced to evaluate the relative accuracy of the two parallel texts of the B account which are found in II Kings 18ff. and Isa. 36ff. As a form critic we judged that the B² account was cast in a legendary form whose historical content was far removed from the historical events of the invasion. The biblical critic does not merely describe a literary situation, but offers value judgments upon the varying elements of the passage.

Then how does this responsibility function when making theological value judgments? The first point is a negative one. The theologian must be critical of the use of norms which may function legitimately in another context when employed as

---

(1958), pp. 144ff.; and Paul Holmer, 'Metaphysics and Theology: The Foundations of Theology', *Lutheran Quarterly* 17 (1965), pp. 309ff.

theological criteria. For example, it does not follow that a norm for fixing historical accuracy or chronological priority can also serve to determine theological value. The B² account is of less value than B¹ for the historian who wishes to understand the eighth-century events, but in terms of the theological relation of the two accounts there is no necessary carry-over. The same case holds for the use of form critical norms. Categories such as annal, legend, midrash should carry no theological bias, whether positive or negative. Nor is there any justification for assuming a dogmatic norm according to which the prophetic stance toward Assyria is judged favourably and even assigned a revelatory significance, while every other position is evaluated in accordance with this norm. In terms of the Assyrian crisis, the variant role of Isaiah which is pictured in B¹ in comparison to that of the oracles does not necessarily lead to the conclusion that B¹ is a theological distortion. Finally, this restriction applies in the same way to the use of psychological, existential, or *heilsgeschichtliche* norms which may, or may not, have a legitimacy within another context.

The case which is being defended is that of the autonomous nature of theological norms. Because a criterion of judgment functions in one context, it does not follow that such may have a similar role in deducing theological evaluations. However, the argument is not being advanced that the norms of the theological discipline necessarily operate in complete isolation from those of the other contexts. The exact relation must be established and could vary from situation to situation.

What then can be said in a positive sense regarding the use of theological norms when faced with biblical diversity? Initially, the importance of this question in the light of the present state of biblical studies should not be overestimated. The concern to deal theologically with the diversity must follow the detailed and careful examination of texts with the appropriate descriptive disciplines. Much fruitless energy has been spent on such theological issues when the urgent need lies in carrying through the preliminary descriptive tasks. The tremendous contribution of von Rad's *Old Testament Theology* is, above all, in his sensitive and precise hearing of Israel's traditions and in describing their development with such clarity.

If the problem of using theological norms within the Old

Testament is seen as a final and even modest stage of exegesis, then several suggestions can be made. First, the theological problem of diversity is not merely a modern question, but can be shown to have already emerged within the Old Testament itself. This means that one cannot avoid the issue by claiming it to be a false problem which would disappear if the modern theologian would 'think Hebraically'. Moreover, it is apparent that no one solution was employed to meet the problem by all who were involved. When accused of inconsistency in his message, Isaiah defended himself by appealing to the diversity in the plan of God, which changed like the farmer's activity according to the season (28.23ff.). Diversity, even if seemingly contradictory, was demanded by the nature of the divine purpose. However, the problem of diversity was met by the Chronicler in quite another way. His method was to harmonize the tension by selection or omission. This state of affairs within the Old Testament should effect caution against seeking a single correct approach.

Secondly, the problem of diversity should be viewed at some point in the light of the existing elements of continuity. It is particularly important that the biblical diversity be seen against the background of its ancient Near Eastern setting. This perspective often enables the interpreter to plot a common area within which all the Old Testament diversity functions, and yet distinct or different from the movements of the Near Eastern religions. In terms of the diverse reactions to the Assyrian crisis, there remain many elements which are shared by the majority of the biblical sources. Such themes as Yahweh's ability to direct the affairs of the world, his judgment on Assyria's boastful claims of autonomy, and his demand from Israel of an obedient response, appear throughout most of the Old Testament accounts. The case can be defended that seldom did Israel attempt cultic manipulation or magical incantation to influence the deity in the face of the enemy's threats. Such elements should not be overemphasized nor should they be developed into a system of theological reductionism. To what extent the really significant theological assertions are held in common by all is an important question.

Thirdly, it is possible to establish some relative norms by comparing passages which have similar contexts to see whether a characteristic stance emerges against which the nature of the divergencies may be made more precise. For example, Isaiah's

oracles against the nations have broad parallels in both Amos and
the later, seventh-century prophets. There are many typical elements of accusation and judgment. It might be possible to sketch
some general theological norms for the prophets which functioned
in given situations, and then to chart the differing degrees to
which such norms were actually operative. Similarly, the prophetic
legend was frequently employed in the context of the Dtr.
historian. The parallel situations could bring into focus the theological function of this form for Dtr., and illustrate varying
degrees of theological intensity within a common structure. For
example, a comparison of the role of Elisha and Isaiah toward the
king and the foreign nations in Dtr. might afford an opportunity
for tracing levels of theological seriousness.

Finally, the measuring of the effect of one testimony upon
another would afford some way of determining the dominant
forces within the diversified traditions. It is clear, for example,
that the oracles of Isaiah continued to flow throughout the long
history of transmission and resulted in creating a number of
smaller eddies. The effect of the dominant force can be seen in the
B accounts, in the Chronicler and in the prophetic liturgy. A
similar effect on the tradition cannot be claimed for the annal or
the Dtr. legend. Such an analysis would allow for some evaluation
in regard to the centrality of certain theological currents.

These approaches to theological diversity which we have outlined attempt to find some relative guides from within the tradition itself. Such an enterprise will remain modest and, to some
extent, indecisive because of its very nature. Many biblical
scholars feel strongly that the task of Old Testament interpretation
should end at this point, if not before. Any effort to bring to bear
other norms than those found within the tradition leads either to
uncontrolled subjectivism or arbitrary dogmatism. I do not share
this point of view. Rather, I would argue the position that another
type of theological norm can be developed from within a different
context[8] and to compatible with it.

In the history of exegesis, both classical Judaism and early

[8] The following discussion is a modification of the position which I
expressed in *Interpretation* 18 (1964), pp. 432ff. The phrase 'interpretation in
faith' was misinterpreted by several critics to be a defence of a dogmatic
position which was based on a subjective, privatistic faith. I meant by the
phrase the confession of the Christian Church which affirms both Old and
New Testaments as Scripture.

Christianity approached the Old Testament from within the context of a 'resultant system'.[9] This is to say, the context for interpreting the Old Testament was defined in reference to another set of tradition. For Judaism it was the oral and written tradition of the Synagogue Fathers; for Christianity it was the apostolic witness to Jesus Christ.[10] The essential point to be made is that this approach—and I confine my remarks now to Christianity—did not attempt to establish dogmatically the *content* of the biblical norms. Rather, it lays claim only to the *context* from which the Church sought exegetically to understand the biblical message. Now I am suggesting that such a confessional stance does not necessarily claim to be the only context from which the Old Testament can be read. (It would be ridiculous to make such a claim in the modern age.) Nor does it make irrelevant the need for the interpreter, who takes seriously the Christian canon as his theological context, to understand the Old Testament in its original historical context. However, the claim is being made that the *theological* norms of *Christian* theology can only emerge from the context of Christian Scripture, that is, Old and New Testaments together. The New Testament does not function as a self-contained norm against the Old. Rather, within the context of both Testaments the task of the biblical theologian is to engage in disciplined inquiry, appropriate to the context and material, from which theological judgments are possible. However, to elaborate this thesis would necessitate another monograph.

To summarize: The problem of developing theological norms with which to evaluate the diversity within the Old Testament finally forces the interpreter outside the context of the Old Testament and raises the broader questions of Scripture and canon.

[9] The term is J. Barr's, *op. cit.*, p. 108.

[10] There are obviously many refinements needed at this point, but the present concern is with establishing some main lines in order to clarify the issues at stake.

THE SUMMARY-APPRAISAL FORM

I

THE book of I Isaiah has not received the rigorous form critical analysis which has been directed to many of the other prophets. This failure is due in part to the several splendid commentaries of a past generation which continue to exercise much influence. Nevertheless, it is increasingly evident that many problems in the book were not adequately explained or even fully recognized by the literary critics. The object of this essay is to deal with one such problem.

The fragmentary character of Isa. 14.24-27 had been seen even before Gesenius' commentary (1821), and the attempts to offer a solution have been many. It is evident that there is no organic relation to v. 23, and that v. 28 begins a new unit. Form critically speaking, the initial verses (24-25) are part of a typical threat pattern, introduced by the swear formula of a *Gottesrede*. The real problem, however, arises in connection with verses 26f. The obvious reference to the plan in v. 24 indicates a close connection with what has preceded. What function then does this verse play in the oracle and precisely what is its form?

First of all, there is a change in speakers. The first person of the swear oracle has ended, and Yahweh is addressed in the third person (v. 27). This break is marked by the demonstrative 'this' (*zō'th*) which functions both as a bridge from the threat to v. 26, as well as a signal for a fresh beginning. The tone of the oracle has also changed in v. 26. No longer is a threat being given, but rather a prophetic reflection upon the scope and implications of the threat is offered. The purpose of Yahweh extends beyond Assyria to encompass all the nations of the earth. V. 26 almost serves as a commentary which summarizes and extends the implications of what has preceded. The two rhetorical questions of v. 27 serve in effect as motivation clauses for the appraisal to provide its authorization. The function of vv. 26-27 is both to summarize the oracle: *this* is the purpose, and to evaluate it: it will succeed because it is from Yahweh.

The oracle in Isa. 17.12-14 differs completely in terms of its form and yet it presents a similar problem in its final verse. The author pictures a horde of people descending in attack with the ferocity of the thunderous sea. Since Gunkel's basic discussion, the chaos imagery has been recognized, now in historicized form. The pattern of events is familiar from the Zion tradition: the terrifying threat, and the sudden deliverance. To the statement which registers the deliverance, 'before morning they are no more', is appended a comment. The similarities to 14.26 are to be noted. Again it is the final verse which is attached to an independent oracle and is not an organic part of it. A shift in speakers is again evident. 14b introduces the first person plural for the first time. The prophet's identification with the delivered people points up his role in appraising the event. The demonstrative pronoun (*zeh*) serves a referential role as before and summarizes in a word what has happened.

The strong didactic flavour of 14b again appears, but not in a hortatory sentence or in a direct warning. Rather, the fate of this attacking people becomes a general illustration from which a lesson is drawn. Such will be the fate of all our attackers! The vocabulary used is of interest. 'Portion' (*ḥēleq*) and 'lot' (*gôrāl*) indicate that the destruction is not accidental, but belongs to a larger plan. Finally, the bicolon form of the comment parallels that in 14.26, but without any subsequent motivation clause.

Chapter 28 is a collection of oracles which were delivered at varying times to different audiences. Nevertheless, there are many indications of redactional activity which would join the oracles thematically. Just as the proud drunkards of Ephraim disregarded their warning and were destroyed, so will the scoffers in Judah fall. It still remains a difficult and much debated problem to understand how the parable in 23-29 fits into this disputational framework.[1] Because there is no direct application, the exact point of the passage is left somewhat up in the air. The prophet seems to be disputing by analogy the claim that Yahweh's purpose

---

[1] Cf. S. C. Thexton, 'A Note of Isaiah xxviii, 25 and 28', *VT* 2 (1952), pp. 81f., and L. J. Liebreich, 'The Parable taken from the Farmer's Labors in Isa. 28.23-29' (Hebrew), *Tarbiz* 24/2 (1955), pp. 126ff.

is strange and inconsistent. If the farmer derives from God his knowledge of the proper season and appropriate skill, how much greater must Yahweh's wisdom be. It has an inner logic like the farmer's which knows how to match the right action to the moment.

The *mashal* begins with a prophetic call to attention, which introduces the two parallel parts of the unit. The first part (24-25) raises a number of questions which would evoke ready answers from the listeners concerning familiar agricultural practices. V. 26 draws the necessary conclusion that the farmer is taught this knowledge by God. The second section (26-28) makes a slightly different, but parallel point with the emphasis falling more on the appropriate method than on the season. V. 29 then draws the didactic implications similar to v. 26. The connective 'also this' (*gam-zeh*) serves to order the farmer's skill in the second part of the parable with that of the first.

In spite of the fact that the final verse unifies the two parts of the parable, it fits into a formal pattern which has not been simply shaped by the inner structure of the parable. V. 26 draws its lesson by means of quite a different form than does v. 29. We are suggesting that v. 29 is another example of the summary-appraisal form which still relates organically to the parable, but stands apart as an independent reflection on the wisdom of God. The form summarizes the entire parable along with bringing an appraisal. The final bicolon is not liturgical in character, but reflects the technical language of the sage, whose praise of Yahweh is no less intense than the Psalmist's.

To summarize: Our study of three oracles of Isaiah, which differ in structure and tradition, attempted to show the great similarity in a concluding formal element. In each case the sentence is attached to the end of an oracle as a prophetic word which offers both a summary and an appraisal of what has been said. In each case, the phrase is characterized by a demonstrative pronoun, or similar, which establishes a reference, but also serves as a marker for the independent appraisal. The tone of the comment is didactic without being directly hortatory.

It may serve to make the nature of the form more precise if it is contrasted with other forms of expressions in Isaiah which bear some similarity. The summary-appraisal form is to be distinguished from the concluding hortatory sentence in 2.5 which addresses itself to the people and urges a course of action. Nor is it a confession in the mouth of the people (12.2; cf. Pss. 48.15; 118.23). The form is a prophetic oracle and does not appear in the mouth of Yahweh (54.17) or the nations (20.6). While reference is made to the main oracle, the form itself is not connected syntactically in a causal relationship (8.10). Again, the phrase is not the concluding part of an extended comparison (20.4), but serves an independent, summary role. This latter function distinguishes it from a parenthetical comment such as 28.21. Finally, the didactic, even reflective tone, sets it apart from the summarizing threat, such as is found in the refrain 9.12.

II

The next step in our study must be an investigation of the background of this form. Is it a special creation of Isaiah, or a common feature of all the prophets? First, it is a surprising discovery to find the lack of close parallels in the other prophets. Naturally, the prophets summarize at times as in Isa. 54.17, but the verse is part of a Yahweh speech and lacks the element of appraisal. The form and vocabulary of Jer. 31.25 at first appear to offer a close parallel, but upon closer analysis, serve a different function in the passage. V. 25 pronounces the judgment in a Yahweh speech which is then grounded in the subsequent verses. Again, Isa. 47.14-15 is an extended comparison and not a summary-appraisal form, although there are certain elements in common. The basic difference can be seen from the structure. The comparison form begins with an observation usually taken from nature: stubble is helpless to resist consuming fire. Then a comparison is drawn with human behaviour: so also are those with whom you have laboured. Finally, an appraisal is offered: they are confused and unable to save you. Although there are instances of the summary-appraisal which also contain elements of comparison, the clear distinction between the two forms should be maintained. We conclude that the summary-appraisal form is not common prophetic property.

Nevertheless, in spite of this evidence there are other factors which should restrain anyone from drawing the conclusion too quickly that Isaiah created the form *de novo*. It is always possible that the form could have arisen in Israel's liturgy and was later copied and adapted by the prophet. Although theoretically possible, such a theory is highly unlikely in this case. We noticed the completely uncultic tone of the comment which sets it apart markedly from typical cultic phrases. Indeed, it is the reflective tone with its didactic flavour which would first suggest the area of wisdom literature as a possible setting for the form. Moreover, the obvious concentration of technical wisdom terminology would point in the same direction. Notice, for example, 'the purpose which is purposed' (*hā'ēṣāh hayyeʿûṣāh*-14.26), the 'portion and lot' (*ḥēleq- gôrāl*-17.14), the 'wonderful in counsel and excellent in wisdom' (*hiphlî' 'ēṣāh highdîl tûšiyyāh*-28.29). It is, therefore, logical to turn to the wisdom literature to see if this area offers closer parallels.

In the book of Proverbs there is only one verse which provides a close parallel:

> Such is the (end) of all who get gain by violence,
> It takes away the life of its possessor (1.19).

This verse concludes the section from vv. 10-19. Delitzsch[2] characterizes it as an *epiphonema*, that is, 'a striking reflection which sums up or concludes a discourse' (Webster's *Unabridged Dictionary*). The particle *kēn* serves as a demonstrative and refers specifically to the misfired plans of the wicked in v. 18. The line is a bicolon in which *b* further elucidates the succinct formulation of *a*. The verse generalizes on the fate of all who act in such wickedness. The lesson which he draws is not in the form of a warning directed to the wicked, but rather a general didactic statement which seeks to find a universal element. Prov. 6.29 shares some of these elements, but is in its form an extended comparison rather than a summary-appraisal.

Another parallel appears in Ps. 49.14 (Engl. 13):

> This is the fate of those who have foolish confidence,
> The (end of those) who are pleased with their portion.

Ps. 49 belongs to the category of wisdom psalms. The author reflects with some comfort on death as the 'great equalizer' (Gunkel) of the rich and the poor. It is folly for the rich to suppose that they can avoid the pit because of possessions. The grave will finally claim all men forever. Syntactically, there is a

[2] F. Delitzsch, *Biblical Commentary on the Proverbs of Solomon*, I (Edinburgh, 1874), p. 66.

problem as to how to understand the pronoun *zeh* (this) in v. 14. Does it refer to what has just preceded, or is it used emphatically and points to what follows? Commentators have often been divided in their opinion. I am inclined to accept the latter alternative and see it refers to what follows. The parallel verses in vv. 13 and 21 provide the main division markers. The whole psalm makes one point with obvious repetition. Regardless of the syntax, the verse summarizes and generalizes a wisdom teaching into a more universal formulation. The reflective, almost philosophical tone, is not restricted to the summary, but is shared by the whole psalm.

The book of Job offers several interesting parallels:

> Such is the fate of all who forget God,
> The hope of the impious will perish (8.13).

> Surely such are the dwellings of the ungodly,
> Such is the place of one who does not know God (18.21).

> This is the portion of a wicked man,
> The heritage decreed for him by God (20.29).

> This is the wicked man's portion with God,
> The tyrant's inheritance from the Almighty (27.13).

The striking similarity of these verses to one another is immediately evident. In each case, the sentence concludes a speech or section of a speech by one of Job's friends, rather than Job himself.[3] Each time an adverbial particle makes reference to the oracle which has preceded. Each time the bicolon form is used. Again, the sentence not only summarizes the argument, but attempts to draw a larger principle from the instances cited which will include that of Job by inference. The fate of a class of wicked is delineated, and the inevitable judgment pronounced, not as a direct threat, but as sound wisdom.

In 5.17ff. Eliphaz characterizes the lot of the man who submits to God's reproof. 'For he wounds, but he binds up . . . you shall know that your tent is safe . . . you shall come to your grave in ripe old age.' In 5.27 he summarizes his point, commends it to Job, and even expands it to form a homily.

> Lo, this we have searched out; it is true.
> Now hear it, know it yourself.

---

[3] There is a problem in 27.13, but the majority of commentators are agreed that this verse is part of Zophar's missing speech.

In spite of the positive content and the expansion into a paraenetic style, the basic form is the same. A principle of human behaviour has been discerned from experience. The sage characterizes it, appraises it as true, and in so doing commends it as the course of wisdom.

Finally, the book of Ecclesiastes abounds in parallels, and yet the tensions within the book itself and the subtlety of the material should caution one against any quick equations. There is a marked shift in the perspective of Qoheleth from that articulated by the friends of Job. While Qoheleth speaks much of his searching for principles of understanding—how to know wisdom and folly— the results are chiefly negative. Rather than discerning any general structures of wisdom, his book consists chiefly in critical judgments on the accepted principles. Galling's[4] insight is a fundamental one: the author stands fully within the traditional school of wisdom, but at key points he offers his own sceptical criticism of the tradition. The basic shift is away from generalization to critical appraisal.

Qoheleth's method of research is thoroughly consistent with the school of wisdom. The sage gathers evidence through his experience, and from his findings seeks to discern the ways of truth and falsehood. So Qoheleth 'sees' ($r'h$), he 'hears' ($šm'$), he 'searches' ($drš$), he 'investigates' (twr), he 'gathers' ($'sp$), he 'makes' ($'šh$). To this mass of data is added the crucial process of reflection. This activity is described fully in a passage, 7.23ff.:

All this I have tested by wisdom . . . I turned my mind to know and to search out and to seek wisdom and the sum of things. . . . Behold, this is what I found . . . adding one thing to another to find the sum, which my mind has sought repeatedly. . . .

In a word, this is the classic description of the activity which produces the summary-appraisal form.

Moreover, the book of Ecclesiastes is filled with the formula. Ch. 4 consists in a series of wisdom sayings which are reminiscent of the older aphorisms of Proverbs, but to this is added notes of critical appraisal. The anomaly of the rich man without family or friends, who never ceases to increase his wealth through continued hard toil, is judged to be folly: 'This also (*gam zeh*) is vanity and an unhappy business' (v. 8). The form of this appraisal is

⁴ K. Galling, 'Kohelet-Studien', *ZAW* 50 (1932), pp. 276ff.

familiar. The demonstrative lumps a variety of activities together, arranges them within a larger category of 'this also', and evaluates it in a two-part sentence. Much of the rest of the book of Ecclesiastes consists in a description of an area of life, whether the pursuit of knowledge, or the search for fame, or the desire of pleasure, or the satisfaction of work, which is then summarized and appraised. The stereotyped nature of the appraisal as 'vanity' should not obscure the real nature of the form. Moreover, in several cases a positive summary-appraisal form appears. In 2.14 the form is followed by a motivation clause. In 5.18 it appears as a parenthetical comment.

The widespread occurrence of the summary-appraisal form within the Old Testament wisdom literature would lead one to suspect that the formula is not confined to the Bible, but is characteristic of Near Eastern wisdom literature in general. Moreover, a study of the major wisdom collections from Egypt[5] does reveal some similarities. Frequently there is appended to the conclusion of a collection of wisdom sayings a summary statement. So, for example, the Instruction for King Merikare[6] concludes: 'Behold, I have spoken to thee the profitable matters of my belly. . . .' Or, the Instructions of King Amenemopet[7]: 'Behold, the thirty chapters. . . ' Or, the Teachings of Cheti[8]: 'Behold, these things, I (have set them) before thee and thy children's children.' Occasionally along with the summary is found some statement akin to an appraisal. Thus in Amenemopet[9]: 'Behold, the thirty chapters, they entertain, they instruct, they are the foremost of all books. They make the ignorant to know. . . .' Sirach concludes with the statement which includes both elements of the form: 'More such things we might say, and not attain the end. And the sum of the matter: He is all' (43.27). However, in the majority of cases in ancient wisdom literature the summary formula does not lead to an appraisal, but into a typical exhortation. So in the Instructions of Amenemopet[10]: 'Fill thyself with them, put them in thy heart.'

Both in terms of form and content, it is impossible to see any close parallel in the above examples. The concluding phrases are

---

[5] Cf. the excellent bibliography by J. Leclant, *Les Sagesses du Proche-Orient* (Paris, 1963), pp. 18ff.
[6] *ANET*², p. 418.   [7] *Ibid.*, p. 424.   [8] *Ibid.*, p. 434.
[9] *Ibid.*, p. 424.   [10] *Ibid.*

addressed to the contents of a book or literary collection, rather than as a summary of the subject matter itself which is the case for the biblical material. This means that in spite of some general similarity, a close parallel in the extra-biblical material to the summary-appraisal form does not appear. The biblical form bears the particular stamp of Hebrew wisdom.

To summarize: We suggest that the evidence offers enough significant parallels within the Old Testament to allow one to draw the conclusion that Isaiah is dependent on a traditional form which had its setting within a Hebrew school of wisdom. This conclusion confirms, from a small area, the interpretation of Isaiah[11] as having a special affinity to the wise men of Israel. However, until our knowledge of the background of Old Testament wisdom is considerably widened, it will be difficult to delineate further how the form was used, or why it is missing in the older proverbial material.

[11] J. Fichtner, 'Jesaja unter den Weisen', *TLZ* 74 (1949), pp. 75ff.

Excursus II

TEXT CRITICAL PROBLEMS IN
II KINGS 18-19 (ISAIAH 36-37)

OLD Testament scholars have long recognized that the parallel passage in Kings and Isaiah raises a whole battery of text critical questions. The first thorough examination of these problems in the modern period was carried out by Gesenius (1821), and his remarkable study remained basic for all subsequent treatments. He concluded that the Isaiah passage had been borrowed from Kings, that the Isaiah text had been abbreviated in the process, and that the Kings text was to be preferred. With few exceptions (Olmstead, Montgomery) his conclusions have been accepted (Kuenen, Driver, Burney, etc.). However, in the light of the recent revival of text critical interest which has been evoked by the new manuscript evidence from the Judaean desert, the traditional approach is no longer adequate. In fact, it is obvious that the entire field is in flux and that new solutions will have to wait until the full publication and study of the evidence.

However, it seems of value to re-examine Gesenius' conclusions if only to raise questions regarding them. First, Gesenius defended the thesis that the Hebrew text of Isaiah had been borrowed from Kings. This hypothesis was advanced as part of the larger question concerning the composition of the book of Isaiah. The traditional position, which was based on the supposition that the eighth-century prophet was directly responsible for the formation of the book of Isaiah, maintained that chs. 36-39 had also been composed on the basis of historical information from the prophet himself. Gesenius contested this, arguing that in II Kings 18ff. the account has an integral part in the book, whereas in the book of Isaiah it functions as an appendage. As additional evidence he produced the textual argument. The close similarity of the parallel texts—in striking contrast to II Sam. 22 and Ps. 18— confirmed his conclusion of literary dependence of one upon the other. To state the issue in terms of the recent discussion, the texts are of one text type and do not evidence a long history of independent textual development. The force of this argument is seen when one contrasts this situation with the textual tradition of the Chronicler, especially if Cross is correct in his theory of local text types.[1] There is no evidence to indicate that originally different text types were secondarily made to conform by the evolving Masoretic tradition. Naturally, the problem of the relation of the Masoretic tradition to its *Vorlage* is not touched by recognizing that both Kings and Isaiah underwent a similar recensional development of the Hebrew text. To this extent, the first thesis of Gesenius still seems sound.

The second thesis that the excesses in the Hebrew text of Kings over Isaiah has resulted from an abbreviation in the latter raises innumerable problems. Gesenius argued that the shorter Isaiah text arose from the conscious omission of superfluous and clumsy expressions. However, the criteria for determining whether the excess was in fact abbreviation by Isaiah or expansion in Kings remained unclear. Already fifty years ago, Olmstead[2] challenged Gesenius' thesis in a pioneer essay and argued for a post-LXX date for the last general revision of Kings. Then Orlinsky[3] was able to demonstrate convincingly the post-LXX expansion in at least four important cases which supported the recensional direction set out by Olmstead.

The crucial issue in all this discussion turns on the question of how to evaluate the LXX Here the evidence from the scrolls of the Judaean desert has been epoch-making. In a brilliant synthesis Cross has begun to sketch some main lines of the recensional history of the biblical text.[4] Basic is the observation that the *Vorlage* of the Greek text for the Books of Kingdoms is not identical with the proto-Masoretic text tradition. Rather, the LXX represents a different text type which it closely followed and which underwent a recensional history to bring the Greek Bible into conformity with the evolving Hebrew textual tradition. However, in spite of this tremendous advance in understanding

[1] F. M. Cross, 'The History of the Biblical Text in the Light of Discoveries in the Judean Desert', *HTR* 57 (1964), pp. 281ff.
[2] A. T. Olmstead, 'Source Study and the Biblical Text', *AJSL* 30 (1913), pp. 1-35; and 'The Earliest Book of Kings', *AJSL* 31 (1915), pp. 169-214.
[3] H. M. Orlinsky, 'The Kings-Isaiah Recensions of the Hezekiah Story', *JQR* 30 (1939-40), pp. 33-49.
[4] Cross, *op. cit.*

in some areas, the problem of evaluating the Greek text of Isaiah remains unsolved. The difficulty of the problem is evident in analysing the parallel text of Isa. 36-39 // II Kings 18-20. The Kings, Greek is a slavishly literal translation as one would now expect in the *kai ge* recension of the Books of Kingdoms,[5] with the minuscules boc$_2$e$_2$ reflecting a Lucian tradition which is prior to this recension.[6] On the other hand, the Greek of Isaiah is a translation[7] which diverges remarkably from the present Masoretic text. Two factors seem clearly at work. First, there is the strong possibility that the Hebrew *Vorlage* of Greek Isaiah differed considerably from the Masoretic tradition.[8] Secondly, the Greek translation gives every sign of being a free translation of the Hebrew text.[9] However, until more evidence is available, it is almost impossible to judge in a given case how to evaluate the weight of the LXX.

A classic example of the difficulty is offered in the variant readings in II Kings 19.9 // Isa. 36.9. Kings reads *wayyāšobb* (he returned, again), while Isaiah has *wayyišmaʿ* (he heard). The Greek Isaiah reads ἀκούσας ἀπέστρεψεν (hearing he returned) and is now supported by the first Isaiah scroll of Qumran (1QIsa^a) which has *wyšmʿ wyšwb*. Scholars are divided on how to interpret this

---

[5] Cf. D. Barthélemy, *Les Devanciers D'Aquila* (Leiden, 1963), and the basic earlier work of H. St J. Thackeray, 'The Greek Translators of the Four Books of Kings', *JTS* 8 (1907), pp. 262ff.

[6] Note in II Kings 18.31 the characteristic handling of the Hebrew noun *ʾiš* (man).

[7] The question of the unity of the translation of Isaiah has been much discussed. Cf. especially J. Ziegler, *Untersuchungen zur Septuaginta des Buches Isaias* (Münster, 1934), pp. 31ff., with his references to Thackeray, Gray, Baumgärtel, and Fischer. Ziegler defends the unity of the translation, although he unfortunately omits discussion of Isa. 36-39 (cf. p. iii). He tries to account for the distinctive differences in the vocabulary of First and Second Isaiah by suggesting that the translator may have used a previous translation as a basis for his own (p. 45). My own study confirmed all the characteristics of the Isaiah translator in chs. 36-39. Decisive is the consistent transliteration of *šĕbhāʾôth* (cf. 37.32 // II Kings 19.31), the rendition of *nṣl* (miphal and hiphil) with ῥύεσθαι against II Isaiah and II Kings ἐξαιρεῖν, and the characteristic handling of ἄνθρωπος, ὀικουμένη, χώρα. This means that the Greek translation of Isa. 36-39 cannot be related to the recensional history of Sam.-Kings.

[8] Cf. J. Ziegler, 'Die Vorlage des Isaias-Septuaginta (LXX) und die erste Isaias-Rolle von Qumran (1QIs^a)', *JBL* 78 (1959), pp. 34ff.

[9] Cf. the instructive list of examples by I. L. Seeligmann, *The Septuagint Version of Isaiah* (Leiden, 1948), p. 42, which could be easily increased (36.5 // II Kings 18.20; 36.16 // 18.31; 37.3 // 19.3).

evidence.[10] Is the LXX simply a conflated reading or does it retain an original tradition which was partially lost in the Masoretic texts of Kings and Isaiah? The decision is usually strongly influenced by one's general evaluation of the fidelity of the Greek translators to their Hebrew *Vorlage*, and a high degree of subjectivity is still involved. Therefore, a definitive solution to this most crucial textual issue is hardly possible without new evidence. Certainly the complexity of the problem is far greater than ever imagined by Gesenius.

The final thesis of Gesenius was that the Kings text was to be generally preferred over the Isaiah text. If the direction of the Kings text has been toward expansion which seems most likely, then Gesenius' last thesis would immediately undergo a modification. However, the question of the preferred reading in a parallel text is an independent issue which must be decided each time on its own merits. It is possible that at a late stage an editor of Isaiah occasionally replaced an ancient grammatical form with a more common substitute (cf. II Kings 19.23 *qṣh* // Isa. 37.24 *qṣw*). The evidence on the whole would seem to indicate that at times Kings has the preferred reading, while at other times it lies with Isaiah.[11] Perhaps in terms of percentage, the Kings text does retain a slight advantage.

[10] Cf. the discussion of Ziegler, *op. cit.*, p. 56, with Milik and Hempel.

[11] For example, the Kings text seems preferable in its readings in 18.20 *'āmartā*; 18.22 *thō'mĕrûn*, while the Isaiah text is better in 36.21 *wayyaḥarîšû*; 37.9 *'al*; 37.17 *šǎlaḥ*, etc.

INDEX OF AUTHORS

INDEX OF REFERENCES